VALUATION
WORKBOOK

Founded in 1807, John Wiley & Sons is the oldest independent publishing company in the United States. With offices in North America, Europe, Australia and Asia, Wiley is globally committed to developing and marketing print and electronic products and services for our customers' professional and personal knowledge and understanding.

The Wiley Finance series contains books written specifically for finance and investment professionals as well as sophisticated individual investors and their financial advisors. Book topics range from portfolio management to e-commerce, risk management, financial engineering, valuation and financial instrument analysis, as well as much more.

For a list of available titles, visit our Web site at www.WileyFinance.com.

VALUATION WORKBOOK

STEP-BY-STEP EXERCISES AND TESTS TO HELP YOU MASTER *VALUATION*

FIFTH EDITION

McKinsey & Company

Tim Koller

Marc Goedhart

David Wessels

Erik Benrud

WILEY

JOHN WILEY & SONS, INC.

Cloth edition: ISBN 978-0-470-42465-0

Cloth edition with DCF Model Download: ISBN 978-0-470-42469-8

University edition: ISBN 978-0-470-42470-4

Workbook: ISBN 978-0-470-42464-3

DCF Model CD-ROM: ISBN 978-0-470-42457-5

DCF Model Download: ISBN 978-0-470-89455-2

Instructor's Manual: ISBN 978-0-470-42472-8

10 9 8 7 6 5 4 3 2

Contents

About the Authors

McKinsey & Company is a management-consulting firm that helps leading corporations and organizations make distinctive, lasting, and substantial improvements in their performance. Over the past seven decades, the firm's primary objective has remained constant: to serve as an organization's most trusted external adviser on critical issues facing senior management.

With consultants deployed from over 80 offices in more than 40 countries, McKinsey advises companies on strategic, operational, organizational, financial, and technological issues. The firm has extensive experience in all major industry sectors and primary functional areas, as well as in-depth expertise in high-priority areas for today's business leaders.

Tim Koller is a partner in McKinsey's New York office. He leads the firm's Corporate Performance Center and is a member of the leadership group of the firm's global corporate finance practice. In his 25 years in consulting Tim has served clients globally on corporate strategy and capital markets, mergers and acquisitions (M&A) transactions, and value-based management. He leads the firm's research activities in valuation and capital markets. He was formerly with Stern Stewart & Company and with Mobil Corporation. He received his MBA from the University of Chicago.

Marc Goedhart is a senior expert in McKinsey's Amsterdam office and leads the firm's Corporate Performance Center in Europe. Over the past 15 years, Marc has served clients across Europe on portfolio restructuring, capital markets, and M&A transactions. He taught finance as an assistant professor at Erasmus University in Rotterdam, where he also earned a PhD in finance.

David Wessels is an adjunct professor of finance at the Wharton School of the University of Pennsylvania. Named by *BusinessWeek* as one of America's top business school instructors, he teaches courses on corporate valuation and private equity at the MBA and executive MBA levels. David is also a director in Wharton's executive education group, serving on the executive development faculties of several Fortune 500 companies. A former consultant with McKinsey, he received his PhD from the University of California at Los Angeles.

Erik Benrud earned his doctorate at the University of Virginia. He is a clinical full professor of finance and the CFA Review Coordinator and Advisor at Drexel University. Erik's publications have appeared in a wide variety of journals, and he has won teaching and research awards from Association to Advance Collegiate Schools of Business (AACSB)-accredited universities. In addition to his many years of teaching, he has done consulting work and delivered seminars on many topics in finance on four continents. He holds the Chartered Financial Analyst (CFA), Financial Risk Manager (FRM), and Chartered Alternative Investment Advisor (CAIA) designations.

Introduction

The purpose of any workbook is to actively engage the reader/learner in the transfer of knowledge from author to reader. Although there are many levels at which knowledge can be transferred, the *Valuation Workbook* endeavors to provide the following three services:

1. A walk-through accompaniment to *Valuation: Measuring and Managing the Value of Companies*, Fifth Edition.
2. A summary of each chapter.
3. Tests of comprehension and skills of many types.

Multiple-choice questions pique your memory as you read the text. Lists and table completions force you to actively rearrange concepts explicitly or implicitly within the text. Calculation questions allow you to apply the skills deployed by the authors in accomplishing the analysis called valuation.

Our aim is to encourage you to question what you read against the background of your own business experience and think about new ways to analyze and approach valuation issues.

VALUATION
WORKBOOK

Part One

Questions

1

Why Value Value?

The chief measures for judging a company are its ability to create value for its shareholders and the amount of total value it creates. Corporations that create value in the long term tend to increase the welfare of shareholders and employees as well as improve customer satisfaction; furthermore, they tend to behave more responsibly as corporate entities. Ignoring the importance of value creation not only hurts the company but leads to detrimental results such as market bubbles.

Value creation occurs when a company generates cash flows at rates of return that exceed the cost of capital, and accomplishing this goal usually requires that the company has a competitive advantage. Activities such as leverage and accounting changes do not create value. Frequently, managers shortsightedly emphasize earnings per share (EPS); in fact, a poll of managers found that most managers would reduce discretionary value-creating activities such as research and development (R&D) in order to meet short-term earnings targets. One method to meet earnings targets is to cut costs, which may have short-term benefits but can have long-run detrimental effects.

1. Data from both Europe and the United States found that the correlation between value creation and employment in the company has been _____ and _____.

2. In the past 30 years there have been at least _____ financial crises that arose largely because companies and banks were _____.

3. Two activities that managers often use in an attempt to increase share price but that do not actually create value are changes in _____ and changes in _____.

4. The conservation of value corollary of the value creation principle says that _____ does not create value.

5. During the Internet boom of the late 1990s, the Microsoft model did not work for many firms because they blindly pursued _____ without _____.

6. The empirical evidence shows that the link between the value created by the acquisition of another company and earnings per share (EPS):

   A. Is strong and positive.

   B. Does not exist.

   C. Is weak and negative.

   D. Is strong and negative.

7. Paying attention to which of the following tends to lead to a company doing well in the stock market?

   I. Cash flow.

   II. Earnings per share.

   III. Growth.

   IV. Return on invested capital.

      A. I and II only.

      B. II and III only.

      C. II, III, and IV only.

      D. I, III, and IV only.

8. Which of the following has *not* been found to occur in companies that adopt long-term value-creation policies?

   A. A smaller, streamlined workforce.

   B. Higher customer satisfaction.

   C. A higher level of corporate responsibility.

   D. Better treatment of former employees.

9. In order to create long-term value, companies must:

   A. Focus on keeping costs at a minimum.

   B. Find the optimal debt-to-equity ratio.

C. Seek and exploit new sources of competitive advantage.

D. Monitor and follow macroeconomic trends.

10. The recent experience with the securitization of risky home loans illustrated how:

    A. Value could be created by the diversification of risk and increased number of investors.

    B. Value could be created by the diversification of risk only.

    C. Value could be created by the increased number of investors only.

    D. Value cannot be created by securitization.

2

Fundamental Principles of Value Creation

Earnings generation and value creation are correlated over the long run, but they are not the same. Value creation is determined by cash flows, which can be disaggregated into revenue growth and return on invested capital (ROIC). For any level of growth, increasing ROIC increases value; however, the reverse is not true. When ROIC is greater than the cost of capital, increasing growth increases the value of the firm; when ROIC is less than the cost of capital, increasing growth decreases the firm's value. When ROIC equals the cost of capital, growth does not affect a firm's value.

For the years 1991 to 2001, General Electric provides a good example of the importance of increasing ROIC. Over the period, revenue increased by only 4 percent per year, but ROIC increased from 13 percent to 31 percent. A $1 investment would have increased to $8 over that time period.

The key value driver formula, also called the "Tao of corporate finance," is:

$$\text{Value} = \frac{\text{NOPLAT}_{t=1} \cdot \left(1 - \frac{\text{growth}}{\text{ROIC}}\right)}{\text{WACC} - \text{growth}}$$

where NOPLAT is the net operating profit less adjusted taxes.

Because the formula assumes the relationships are static, it may not be very useful in practice; however, it does outline the important relationships that determine and drive value. Part Two of the text expands on the formula.

1. Rank the types of growth from highest to lowest, where highest = 1, in terms of the amount of shareholder value each typically creates from the same incremental increase in revenue.

Types of growth	Ranking
A. Increase share in a growing market.	1. _____
B. Expand an existing market.	2. _____
C. Acquire businesses.	3. _____
D. Introduce new products to market.	4. _____

2. What is the general rule a firm should use when deciding whether to repurchase shares?

3. With respect to value creation, define financial engineering.

4. Complete the following sentence concerning the relationships among earnings, cash flow, and value. Earnings and cash flow are often _____, but earnings don't tell the whole story of value creation, and focusing too much on earnings or earnings growth _____ _____.

5. When ROIC is greater than the cost of capital, the relationship between growth and value is _____. When ROIC is less than the cost of capital, the relationship between growth and value is _____. When ROIC equals the cost of capital, the relationship between growth and value is _____.

6. With respect to countries, the core valuation principle is _____, as made evident by the fact that U.S. companies trade _____ companies in other countries.

7. When comparing the effect of an increase in growth on a high-ROIC company and a low-ROIC company, a 1 percent increase in growth will have _____.

8. Because interest expense is tax deductible, share repurchases can have the beneficial effect of _____, but this may not increase share price because _____.

9. Which of the following is true concerning the practice of repurchasing shares when the managers think the price of the stock is low?

   I. It is a proven method to add value.

   II. Managers have a good record in timing the market in this way.

   III. The practice benefits stockholders who do not sell.

   IV. The practice hurts the stockholders who do sell.

   A. I and II only.

   B. I and III only.

   C. II and III only.

   D. III and IV only.

10. If the growth of a company is 2 percent and the ROIC is 10 percent, what is the investment rate?

   A. 2 percent.

   B. 5 percent.

   C. 12 percent.

   D. 20 percent.

11. For a given company, next year's NOPLAT is $300. For the foreseeable future, the growth rate will be 5 percent, the ROIC will be 15 percent, and the weighted average cost of capital (WACC) will be 13 percent. Using the key driver formula, calculate the value of the company.

   A. $1,666

   B. $2,222

   C. $2,500

   D. $2,750

3

The Expectations
Treadmill

The expectations treadmill is the name for a problem faced by high-performing managers who try to meet the high market expectations that result from the high level of performance in recent periods. It's the reason that, in the short term, extraordinary managers may deliver only mediocre total returns to shareholders (TRS). It's also the dynamic behind the adage that a good company and a good investment may not be the same. An example of this is a comparison of the company and stock performance of Wal-Mart and Target over the period 1995–2006. Although Wal-Mart outperformed Target in both revenue growth and ROIC, the annualized TRSs were 15 and 24 percent, respectively. This may be because their P/E ratios were 15 times and 11 times, respectively, which meant that Target's stock had more upside potential.

Decomposing TRS can give better insights into a company's true performance and in setting new targets. There is already the traditional method of decomposing TRS into three parts: (1) percent change in earnings, (2) percent change in P/E, and (3) dividend yield. A clearer picture can be found from breaking TRS into four parts: (1) the value generated from revenue growth net of the capital required to grow, (2) the growth in TRS that would have taken place without the measure in (1), (3) changes in shareholder's expectations about the company's performance as reflected in a measure such as P/E, and (4) the effect of leverage. A more thorough analysis can explain why a small decline in TRS in the short run to adjust expectations may be preferable to desperately trying to maintain TRS through acquisitions and ill-advised ventures.

Use the following financials to answer Questions 1 through 4.

$ million	Base year	1 year later
Invested capital	$200	$206.6
Earnings	$20	$22
P/E	12	12.6
Equity value	240	277.2
Dividends	$10	$12

1. What is the TRS from performance?
   A. −2.0 percent.
   B. −0.5 percent.
   C. 4.5 percent.
   D. 6.7 percent.

2. What is the dividend yield?
   A. 4.2 percent.
   B. 4.8 percent.
   C. 5.0 percent.
   D. 6.0 percent.

3. What is the zero-growth return?
   A. 8.3 percent.
   B. 10.5 percent.
   C. 12.5 percent.
   D. 15.3 percent.

4. What is the TRS?
   A. 14.0 percent.
   B. 15.0 percent.
   C. 15.5 percent.
   D. 20.0 percent.

5. Using the traditional approach, an analyst can break down TRS into two or three components.

List the components in the two-component breakdown:

A. _____

B. _____

List the components in the three-component breakdown:

A. _____

B. _____

C. _____

6. For periods of _____ years or more, it is true that if managers focus on _____, then their interests and the interests of shareholders should be aligned.

7. The detrimental result of the expectations treadmill is that, for firms that have had superior operating and TRS performance, the managers who try to continually meet the higher expectations may engage in detrimental activities such as _____ or _____.

4

Return on Invested Capital

The basic source of value creation is competitive advantage. The following expression expands the expression of ROIC proposed in Chapter 2:

$$\text{ROIC} = \frac{\text{NOPLAT}}{\text{Invested Capital}} = (1 - \text{Tax Rate})\frac{\text{Price per Unit} - \text{Cost per Unit}}{\text{Invested Capital per Unit}}$$

This formula explains how a higher ROIC is the result of a competitive advantage from being able to charge a higher price or being able to produce at a lower cost. The structure-conduct-performance (SCP) framework provides a strategy model for competitive advantage. One of the most widely used approaches in analyzing strategy is Porter's framework, which focuses on threat of entry, pressure from substitute products, bargaining power of buyers, bargaining power of suppliers, and the degree of rivalry among existing competitors. These forces differ widely by industry.

Five pricing advantages and four cost advantages determine overall competitive advantage. The five pricing advantages are innovative products, quality, brand, customer lock-in, and rational price discipline. The four cost advantages are innovative business methods, unique resources, economies of scale, and scalable products/processes. In a competitive economy, the pricing and cost advantages can erode through competition, and the sustainability of the high ROIC from a competitive advantage depends on issues such as the length of the life cycle of the business and the potential for renewing products. The evidence shows that the relative ROIC of a firm to the average of all other firms and to the firms in the industry remains fairly sustainable for periods of 10 years or more; however, there will be some reversion to the median and/or mean.

1. List Michael Porter's five forces:

   A. _____

   B. _____

   C. _____

   D. _____

   E. _____

2. The key driver of ROIC is _____.

3. According to empirical studies over the past five decades, how successful have firms been in sustaining their rates of ROIC?

4. Explain what quality means in the context of competitive advantage and ROIC.

5. For a pricing advantage, using rational pricing discipline requires either a _____ or _____.

6. Explain the difference between economies of scale and scalable products.

7. Between 1963 and 2008, the median ROIC was _____ percent, and the interquartile range was _____ percent to _____ percent.

8. Compared to the stability of rates of growth, rates of ROIC tend to _____.

9. From highest to lowest, rank the following three industries based on ROIC. They have been selected based on branding advantages and barriers to entry.

A. Computers and peripherals	1. _____
B. Pharmaceuticals	2. _____
C. Paper packaging	3. _____

10. If a firm establishes itself as a high-ROIC firm, within 10 years it is expected that the ROIC will:

    A. Have fallen to the average or be below the average ROIC.

    B. Have fallen, but will still be above the average ROIC.

    C. Not have fallen, and will maintain about the same.

    D. Have continued to trend up.

11. Given that a company charges $3.40 per unit, has a cost per unit of $1.80, has a tax rate of 32 percent, and requires $16 of invested capital per unit, what is the ROIC?

    A. 6.8 percent.

    B. 10.2 percent.

    C. 15.6 percent.

    D. 30.3 percent.

12. Cereal manufacturers can brand their products, but meat producers cannot do so. Based on this fact, which of the following is the most accurate concerning the pricing advantage that cereal manufacturers have over meat producers?

    A. The ROIC for cereal manufactures is less than that of meat producers because branding does not create value and branding has a cost.

    B. The ROIC for cereal manufactures is equal to that of meat producers because the costs and benefits reach an equilibrium.

    C. The ROIC for cereal manufactures is twice as high as that of meat producers.

    D. The ROIC for cereal manufactures is three times as high as that of meat producers.

5

Growth

Growth can vary greatly across industries and across firms within industries. There are three components of revenue growth: (1) portfolio momentum, (2) market share performance, and (3) mergers and acquisitions. Components (1) and (2) are types of organic growth. Components (1) and (3) have the highest explanatory power. In other words, high growth depends more on choosing the right markets and acquisitions and less on gaining market share.

The highest value-creating strategy is entering into fast-growing markets that take revenue from distant companies instead of rivals in the local industry. Other value-creating strategies include developing new products or services, persuading customers to increase the use of the existing products, and attracting new customers.

Trying to increase market share in a growing market may have some success, but it will probably fail to create value in a mature market because of the reactions of rivals. Product promotions, pricing promotions, and incremental product changes rarely create lasting value.

Since products have natural life cycles, sustaining growth is more difficult than sustaining ROIC. To sustain growth, a firm must consistently develop new products in a timely fashion. A study of publicly traded companies found that over the period 1963 to 2007, the median revenue growth rate was 5.4 percent, and the range of the growth rates was 0.9 percent to 9.4 percent. High growth rates decay quickly, and large companies struggle to grow. The median growth of publicly traded companies exceeded that of U.S. gross domestic product (GDP) for three possible reasons: (1) greater access to capital, (2) the effects of outsourcing, and (3) expansion into foreign markets.

1. Identify the sources of organic growth and indicate which has the highest explanatory power for growth.

2. Explain the importance of incremental innovation in creating value.

3. With respect to product development, growth is difficult to maintain because for each product _____, the company must _____. This is called the _____ effect.

4. How has the growth of publicly traded companies in the United States compared to the growth of U.S. GDP?
   Explain the two reasons for the difference.

   A. _____

   B. _____

5. Which of the following is most accurate concerning the revenue growth rates of firms over the years 1963 to 2007?
   A. The range was 1.5 percent to 12 percent, with a median of 7.2 percent.
   B. The range was 0.9 percent to 9.4 percent, with a median of 5.4 percent.
   C. The range was 2.2 percent to 8.8 percent, with a median of 4.2 percent.
   D. The range was –0.2 percent to 6.6 percent, with a median of 3.3 percent.

6. For firms that enter the Fortune 50, which of the following is most accurate concerning the revenue growth rate for the years 2 to 15 after they enter the Fortune 50?
   A. The average revenue growth rate is 1 percent because they are usually large firms.
   B. The average revenue growth rate is 4 percent because they are usually the most efficient firms.
   C. The average revenue growth rate is 4 percent because they are usually large firms.
   D. The average revenue growth rate is 1 percent because they are usually the most efficient firms.

7. Companies that grow faster than 20 percent in one year generally within five years see their growth decline to:

   A. About 4 percent and then down to 2 percent within 10 years.

   B. About 6 percent and then down to 3 percent within 10 years.

   C. About 7 percent and then down to 3 percent within 10 years.

   D. About 8 percent and then down to 5 percent within 10 years.

8. Which of the following explain the reasons that growth-rate rankings change among industries so much over time?

  I. The business cycle.

  II. Changing regulations.

  III. Fluctuating exchange rates.

  IV. Product life cycles.

    A. I and II only.

    B. I and IV only.

    C. II and III only.

    D. III and IV only.

9. Which of the following is true concerning an increase in market share that comes at the expense of established competitors?

   A. It rarely creates much value for long except when it results in pushing a competitor out of the market completely.

   B. It generally creates value for a fairly long period, but it will decay after about 10 years.

   C. It never creates any value over the long run because the effects are random across firms and net to zero for any given firm over time.

   D. None of these.

10. Which of the following usually result in above-average value creation?

  I. Make large acquisitions.

  II. Attract new customers into the market.

  III. Convince existing customers to buy more of a product.

  IV. Make bolt-on acquisitions to accelerate product growth.

    A. I and II only.

    B. I, III, and IV only.

    C. II and III only.

    D. III and IV only.

6

Frameworks for Valuation

Two popular methods for estimating the value of a company are the discounted cash flow (DCF) model and the discounted economic-profit model. Both methods use WACC in the discounting process, and both should give the same estimate. They are appropriate if the capital structure is expected to remain stable; but if the capital structure will change, then the adjusted present value (APV) model is a good alternative. Alternatives to discounted cash flow models include using multiples and real-option models.

To value the firm's equity using the DCF model, an analyst estimates the value of the operating assets, adds the value of nonoperating assets (e.g., cash), and then subtracts the value of debt. An estimate of the value of operations requires a reorganization of financial statements; an analysis of historical performance; a projection of revenue growth, ROIC, and free cash flow; an estimate of continuing value (CV); and an appropriate discount rate.

Economic-profit-based valuation models have the advantage of providing insights into the yearly performance. One formula for economic profit is:

$$\text{Economic Profit} = \text{NOPLAT} - (\text{Invested Capital} \times \text{WACC})$$

If economic profit grows at a constant rate, the value of a firm can be expressed as:

$$\text{Value}_0 = \text{Invested Capital}_0 + \text{Economic Profit}_1/(\text{WACC} - g)$$

If forecasts predict that the capital structure of a firm will change (e.g., the firm pays down debt over time), the adjusted present value (APV) model is the best choice. The APV model uses the following breakdown to value the firm:

$$\text{Adjusted Present Value} = \text{Enterprise Value as If All-Equity Financed}$$
$$+ \text{Present Value of Tax Shields}$$

The first component of APV, the enterprise value as if the company were all-equity financed, is determined by discounting the cash flows using the unlevered cost of equity.

1. The estimate of a firm's present value (PV) of free cash flows (FCFs) is $400 million. Its estimated invested capital is $700 million. It has cash holdings of $9 million. The value of debt and capitalized operating leases are $220 million and $33 million, respectively. If there are 2 million shares of common equity outstanding, what is the estimated value of each share?

2. A firm's estimated present value of economic profit is $150 million. Its estimated invested capital is $250 million. It has cash holdings of $16 million. The value of debt and capitalized operating leases are $80 million and $26 million, respectively. What is the estimated value of equity?

3. Which of the following valuation methods does *not* assume the WACC is constant?

   A. The discounted cash flow model.

   B. The economic-profit model.

   C. The adjusted present value model.

   D. None of these. They all assume the WACC is constant.

4. Which of the following is *not* a nonequity claim that will lower the value of the firm?

   A. Tax loss carried forward.

   B. Unfunded retirement liabilities.

   C. Preferred stock.

   D. Minority interest.

5. The value of a firm's invested capital is $300 million. Its return on invested capital is 12 percent, and its WACC is 10.5 percent. What is the economic profit?

6. Explain the relationship of the adjusted present value model to the Modigliani and Miller proposition concerning the effect of a firm's capital structure on the value of the firm.

7. Complete the table:

Source of capital	Proportion of total capital	Cost of capital	Marginal tax rate	After-tax cost of capital	Contribution to WACC
Debt	42%	6.2%	34%	_____	_____
Equity	58%	9.8%		_____	_____
WACC					_____

8. For the next period, a firm's free cash flow (CF) and its interest tax shield (TS) are estimated to be $40 million and $9 million, respectively. Their growth rates are estimated to be 5 percent and 3 percent, respectively. The unlevered cost of equity is 9 percent and the cost of debt is 6 percent. The levered cost of equity is 12 percent. Using the capital cash flow model, what is the estimated value of the firm?

9. Fill in the following table to calculate equity value. The discount rate is 9 percent. (Hint: See Exhibit 6.14 in the text.)

Year	Free cash flow	Interest tax shield	Discount factor	PV of free CF	PV of interest TS
2011	402	31			
2012	420	32			
2013	436	34			
Continuing value	8,900	380			
Present value					
PV of free cash flow					
PV of interest tax shield					
PV of free cash flow and interest tax shield					
Midyear adjustment factor					622
Value of operations					
Value of long-term investments					155
Value of tax loss carry-forwards					81
Enterprise value					
Value of debt					2,583
Value of capitalized operating leases					1,674
Equity value					

7

Reorganizing the Financial Statements

A proper assessment of financial performance requires reorganizing financial statements to avoid traps like double counting, omitting cash flows, and hiding leverage. A key measure of economic performance is net operating profit less adjusted taxes (NOPLAT), because ROIC = NOPLAT/(Invested capital), and FCF = NOPLAT + Noncash operating expenses − Investments in invested capital.

Other important measures are:

Invested Capital = Operating Assets − Operating Liabilities = Debt + Equity

and

$$
\begin{aligned}
\text{Total Funds Invested} &= \text{Invested Capital} + \text{Nonoperating Assets} \\
&= (\text{Debt and Debt Equivalents}) \\
&\quad + (\text{Equity and Equity Equivalents})
\end{aligned}
$$

In practice, there are difficulties in categorizing assets as operating or non-operating and right-hand balance sheet items as debt or equity, and this makes computing the values in these equations difficult. The analyst should not include excess cash in invested capital because it is not necessary for core operations, and including it will depress ROIC. Also, if a company has financial subsidiaries, the operations of those subsidiaries require a separate analysis from those of the manufacturing operations, because financial institutions have different capital and leverage norms.

Advanced analytical issues include operating leases, pensions and other retirement benefits, capitalized research and development, and nonoperating charges and restructuring reserves. An analyst can estimate the implied value of those leased assets that are not capitalized and obtain a more appropriate measure of leverage with the following equation:

$$\text{Asset Value}_{t-1} = (\text{Rental Expense}_t) * [k_d + 1/(\text{Asset Life})]$$

Like excess cash, excess pension assets and pension shortfalls should not be included in invested capital. Research and development should be included in invested capital. Provisions fall into four basic categories: ongoing operating provisions, long-term operating provisions, nonoperating provisions, and income-smoothing provisions. Each requires an adjustment to return or invested capital or both.

1. How will an increase in invested capital affect FCF and ROIC if all other things are kept equal?
   A. It will decrease both FCF and ROIC.
   B. It will increase both FCF and ROIC.
   C. It will increase FCF but decrease ROIC.
   D. It will decrease FCF but increase ROIC.

2. Which of the following are sources of financing?
   I. Equity equivalents.
   II. Debt equivalents.
   III. Hybrid securities.
   IV. Minority interest.
       A. I and II only.
       B. I, II, and III only.
       C. III and IV only.
       D. I, II, III, and IV.

3. For which of the following would the tax assets and liabilities *not* be included in operating deferred-tax assets or liabilities?
   A. Accelerated inventory deduction.
   B. Goodwill and other intangibles.
   C. Accrued self-insurance liabilities.
   D. State income taxes.

4. Which of the following is a correct equation for tax loss carry-forwards?
   A. Net operating losses minus other accrued liabilities.
   B. Net operating losses plus valuation allowances.

C. Net operating losses plus other accrued liabilities.

D. Net operating losses plus other deferred tax liabilities.

5. For a given leased asset using an operating lease, the rental expense will be $5,000 in the next period. The pretax cost of debt is 8 percent, and the asset has an expected life of five years. When adjusting the balance sheet for estimating value, what would be the estimated asset value of the leased asset in the current period?

A. $12,500

B. $50,000

C. $17,857

D. $38,462

6. A balance sheet has the following entries: cash = $200, receivables = $100, short-term deferred tax assets = $50, and short-term deferred tax liabilities = $30. Based on this information, what is the value of operating current assets?

A. $250

B. $300

C. $320

D. $350

7. According to FASB Statement 158 under U.S. Generally Accepted Accounting Principles (GAAP), with respect to pension value shortfalls and excess pension assets, which are reported directly on the balance sheet?

A. The present value of pension value shortfalls only.

B. The present value of both pension value shortfalls and excess pension assets.

C. The undiscounted value of pension value shortfalls only.

D. The undiscounted value of pension value shortfalls and the present value of pension assets.

8. Given the following balance sheet entries, compute the debt and the total funds invested.

Operating assets = $400	Accounts payable = $60
Marketable securities = $100	Prepaid pension assets = $50
Deferred taxes = $30	Common stock = $200

9. Given the following accounting income statement on the left, enter the appropriate entries into the NOPLAT worksheet on the right. The marginal tax rate is 30 percent.

Revenues	$2,000	Revenues	$2,000
Operating costs	(1,000)	Operating costs	(1,000)
Depreciation	(400)	Depreciation	(400)
Operating profit	$600	Operating profit	$600
Interest	(40)	Operating taxes	_____
Nonoperating income	10	NOPLAT	_____
Earnings before taxes	$570	After-tax nonoperating income	_____
Taxes_____	(171)	Income available to investors	_____
Net income	$399		

10. Given the following financial statements, calculate NOPLAT, working capital, invested capital, and total funds invested.

Income statement	Year	Balance sheet	Year
Revenues	200.0	Working cash	10
Cost of sales	(80.0)	Accounts receivable	30
Selling costs	(50.0)	Inventories	10
Depreciation	(20.0)	Current assets	50
Operating profit	50.0		
		Property, plant, and equipment	150
Interest expense	(4.0)	Prepaid pension assets	5
Gain on sale	–	Total assets	205
Earnings before taxes	46.0		
		Accounts payable	6
Taxes	(13.8)	Short-term debt	12
Net income	32.2	Restructuring reserves	7
		Current liabilities	25
Operating tax rate = 30%		Long-term debt	70
Marginal tax rate = 30%			
		Shareholders' equity	110
		Liabilities and equity	205

8

Analyzing Performance and Competitive Position

The analysis of performance and competitive position begins with an analysis of the key drivers of value: ROIC and revenue growth. After that analysis, an assessment of the financial health of the firm shows whether it can make short-term and long-term investments.

It is useful to analyze ROIC with and without goodwill. Also, the following breakdown of ROIC is a powerful equation in financial analysis:

$$\text{ROIC} = (1 - \text{Operating Cash Tax Rate}) \times \frac{\text{EBIT}}{\text{Revenues}} + \frac{\text{Revenues}}{\text{Invested Capital}}$$

Revenue growth is one of the determinants of cash flows. The analyst should distinguish between organic revenue growth and growth from other factors such as currency effects, acquisitions, or divestitures.

A comprehensive model does a line item analysis, which converts every line in the financial statements into a ratio. Ratios include common size entries computed in terms of assets or revenues for the balance sheet and income statement, respectively, and also days ratios found by the following general expression:

$$\text{Days} = 365 \times \frac{\text{Balance sheet item}}{\text{Revenues}}$$

Other measures provide insights into efficiency relative to other firms. One such expression is a breakdown of labor costs per unit:

$$\frac{\text{Labor Expenses}}{\text{Units of Output}} = \frac{\text{Labor Expenses}/\text{Number of Employees}}{\text{Units of Output}/\text{Number of Employees}}$$

The following equation helps illustrate the power and danger of leverage:

$$ROE = ROIC + [ROIC - (1 - T) \times k_d] \times D/E$$

The analyst should note how the market debt-to-equity ratio compares to peers in terms of the coverage and the level of risk the firm takes.

1. Explain why ROIC is a better analytical tool than return on equity (ROE) and return on assets (ROA).

   ROE: _____

   ROA: _____

2. Which of the following is most accurate?

   A. Analyzing ROIC excluding goodwill is the best measure for determining value added for shareholders.

   B. Analyzing ROIC excluding goodwill serves no purpose.

   C. Analyzing ROIC excluding goodwill is the preferred method for most analysis.

   D. None of these statements are true.

3. Compute ROIC given the following information: EBITDA = $3,000, Revenues = $5,000, Invested capital = $20,000, Operating cash tax rate = 25 percent.

   A. 3.75 percent.

   B. 5.33 percent.

   C. 11.25 percent.

   D. 18.75 percent.

4. Which of the following is the best method of determining if the financial performance between competitors is sustainable?

   A. Linking operating drivers directly to return on capital.

   B. Comparing the respective ROE and ROA measures.

   C. Breaking ROE down into ROIC, tax, interest rate, and leverage effects.

   D. Distinguishing between pretax ROIC and operating-cash tax rate.

5. Which of the following is *not* in the list of conditions where flow return on investment (CFROI) is a preferable measure to ROIC?

A. The firm has lumpy investment patterns.

B. Fixed assets have long lives.

C. The firm uses last-in first-out (LIFO) as opposed to first-in first-out (FIFO) accounting.

D. There is a large ratio of fixed assets to working capital.

6. Given that ROIC, the interest rate on debt, and the debt-to-equity ratio are constant, how will increasing the tax rate affect ROE?

A. Decrease it.

B. Not affect it.

C. Increase it.

D. There is no set relationship.

7. In Exhibit 8.3 in the text, pretax ROIC is broken down into:

A. Operating margin and operating-cash tax rate.

B. Operating margin and revenues divided by invested capital.

C. Operating working capital divided by revenues and fixed assets divided by revenues.

D. Gross margin and selling, general, and administrative (SG&A) expense divided by revenues.

8. Other things being constant, if EBIT and revenues both increase by 10 percent, then it is likely that:

A. ROIC will decrease.

B. ROIC will remain the same.

C. ROIC will increase.

D. ROIC will change, but the direction is not certain.

Use the following data to answer Questions 9 and 10.

	2008	2009
Current assets	$863	$896
Current liabilities	710	818
Debt in current liabilities	1	39
Long-term debt	506	408

	2008	2009
Total assets	2,293	2,307
Capital expenditures	111	117
Change in deferred taxes	−29	−20
Sales	4,056	4,192
Operating expenses	3,307	3,260
Rental expense	0	248
General expenses	562	528
Depreciation	139	136
Interest expense	39	30
Income taxes	5	8

9. For each year, compute the three coverage ratios based on pretax and interest income.

2008	Ratio 1	Ratio 2	Ratio 3
Numerator			
Denominator			
Ratio			

2009	Ratio 1	Ratio 2	Ratio 3
Numerator			
Denominator			
Ratio			

10. If receivables, inventories, and other current assets are $523 in 2008, then what is the number of days in cash?

9

Forecasting Performance

Typically, forecasting involves making projections of cash flows to some point where the company has a steady state going forward characterized by two properties: (1) the company grows at a constant rate with a constant reinvestment ratio, and (2) the company earns a constant rate of return on existing capital and new capital invested. The horizon to the steady state, called the explicit forecast period, is usually 10 to 15 years. The analyst should divide the explicit forecast period into a first forecast period of five to seven years, where the statements will include many details, and the remaining years' forecasts where the statements are simpler with less detail, which avoids the error of false precision. Such forecasts require assumptions concerning a host of variables, including the return earned on invested capital and whether the company can stay competitive.

There are six steps in the forecasting process.

1. Prepare and analyze historical financial statements and data.

2. Build the revenue forecast consistent with historical economy-wide evidence on growth.

3. Forecast the income statement using the appropriate economic drivers.

4. Forecast the balance sheet entries.

5. Forecast the investor funds into the balance sheet.

6. Calculate ROIC and FCF.

Additional issues include determining the effect of inflation, nonfinancial drivers, and which costs are fixed and which are variable.

For Questions 1 through 5, answer True or False.

1. When using plant, property, and equipment (PP&E) as the forecast driver, tie depreciation to net PP&E, rather than using a gross PP&E approach.

2. It is recommended in the financial modeling process to collect raw data on a separate worksheet and record the data as originally reported.

3. The top-down approach cannot be applied to companies in mature industries.

4. The recommended method to forecast taxes is as a percentage of earnings before taxes.

5. To forecast the balance sheet, it is best to first forecast invested capital and nonoperating assets and then forecast excess cash and sources of financing separately.

6. Which of the following is *not* one of the steps in the forecast of individual line items related to the income statement?

   A. Determine the economic relationships that drive the model.

   B. Model the business cycle.

   C. Estimate the forecast ratios.

   D. Forecast the drivers and multiply times the respective ratios.

7. If a company forecasts that its capital expenditures will be smooth, then which is the better method to use for forecasting depreciation: i) using a percentage of revenues or ii) using a percentage of property, plant, and equipment?

   A. Percentage of revenues only.

   B. Percentage of property, plant, and equipment only.

   C. Either method is appropriate because the choice does not matter if expenditures are smooth.

   D. Neither method is appropriate when expenditures are smooth.

8. Which of the following is the best estimate of retained earnings in year T?

   A. Retained earnings$_{T-1}$ + Net income$_{T-1}$ – Dividends$_T$

   B. Retained earnings$_T$ + Net income$_{T-1}$ – Dividends$_{T-1}$

C. Retained earnings$_{T-1}$ + Net income$_T$ − Dividends$_T$

D. Retained earnings$_T$ + Net income$_T$ + Dividends$_T$

9. In industries where prices are changing or technology is advancing, forecasters should:

   A. Use only financial drivers such as revenue.

   B. Use only nonfinancial drivers such as productivity and volume.

   C. Use both financial and nonfinancial drivers.

   D. Use national real aggregates such as real GDP.

10. The value of a steady-state company:

    A. Can be estimated by estimating free cash flow and using the growth perpetuity model.

    B. Can be estimated using the quadratic formula.

    C. Can be estimated using the PP&E method.

    D. Cannot be estimated because at zero growth, the solution involves division by zero.

11. Explain the problem with respect to forecasting cash flows of a parent company that are from investments in subsidiaries where the parent owns less than 20 percent of the subsidiary.

12. List the three steps in making a top-down forecast of revenue:

    A. _____

    B. _____

    C. _____

    List the three inputs for making a bottom-up forecast of revenue:

    A. _____

    B. _____

    C. _____

13. Complete the following table by entering the typical forecast driver in the third column and the typical forecast ratio in the last column.

Typical Forecast Drivers for the Income Statement

	Line item	Typical forecast driver	Typical forecast ratio
Operating	Cost of goods sold (COGS)		
	Selling, general, and administrative expense		
	Depreciation		
Nonoperating	Interest expense		
	Interest income		

14. At the beginning of the year 2009, an analyst has the information in the following table concerning income for 2009. Assume all income is taxed at the same indicated tax rate. The balance sheet assumptions for 2009 are:

   A. Operating cash, excess cash, and equity investments will not change.

   B. Inventory, net PP&E, and accounts payable will increase at the same rate as sales.

   C. Short-term and long-term debt will increase by 10 percent.

   D. The firm will use a residual dividend policy so that all additional financing will come from retained earnings and the rest of earnings will be paid out as a dividend.

   Fill out the table.

	2009	2010		2009	2010
Revenue growth		20%	Revenues	500	600
Cost of goods sold/revenue	40%	40%	Cost of goods sold		
Selling and general expenses/revenues	30%	20%	Selling and general expenses		
Depreciation/net PP&E	20%	30%	Depreciation	(56)	
EBITA/revenues			EBITA		
Interest rate					

(Continued)

(Continued)

	2009	2010		2009	2010
Interest expense	10%	8%	Interest expense	(40)	
Interest income	6%	5%	Interest income	12	
			Nonoperating income	10	
Nonoperating items			Earnings before taxes		
Nonoperating income growth		30%			
			Provision for income taxes	(22.8)	
Taxes			Net income		
Average tax rate	30%	30%			

	2008	2009		2008	2009
Assets			Liabilities and equity		
Operating cash	10		Accounts payable	20	
Excess cash	200		Short-term debt	300	
Inventory	60		Current liabilities	320	
Current assets	270				
			Long-term debt	100	
Net PP&E	280		Common stock	80	
Equity investments	100		Retained earnings	150	
Total assets	650		Total liabilities and equity	650	

10

Estimating
Continuing Value

There are two parts to the estimated value of a company based on future cash flows: (1) a portion of the value based on the initial, explicit forecast period, and (2) a portion of the value based on continuing performance beginning at the end of the explicit forecast period. The continuing value (CV) often exceeds half of the total estimated operating value, and when early years have negative cash flows, the continuing value can exceed the total estimated operating value. There are two formulas for estimating continuing value: (1) the discounted cash flow (DCF) formula and (2) the economic-profit formula. The DCF formula is:

$$CV_t = \frac{NOPLAT_{t+1}\left[1 - \dfrac{g}{RONIC}\right]}{WACC - g}$$

Special considerations in estimating the inputs are that (1) NOPLAT should reflect an average level associated with the midpoint of the business cycle, (2) return on new invested capital (RONIC) should reflect realistic assumptions concerning the level of competition, (3) WACC should be based on a sustainable capital structure, and (4) g should be based on a long-term measure such as the consumption growth for the industry's products.

The economic-profit formula for continuing value is:

$$CV_t = \frac{IC_t\,[ROIC_t - WACC]}{WACC} + \frac{PV\,(\text{Economic Profit}_{t+2})}{WACC - g}$$

$$PV\,(\text{Economic Profit}_{t+2}) = \frac{NOPLAT_{t+1}\left[\dfrac{g}{RONIC}\right](RONIC - WACC)}{WACC}$$

The length of the explicit forecast period does not affect the value of the company. There can be a difference between the return on new invested capital and the return on existing invested capital. Also, there is not necessarily a direct relationship between the size of the estimated continuing value and the actual value created in the continuing value period.

Other methods for estimating continuing value exist. The convergence formula is related to the preceding formulas, for example, and it assumes that excess profits will eventually be competed away. The convergence formula gives the following relationship:

$$CV = \frac{NOPLAT_{t+1}}{WACC}$$

Some methods do not depend on the time value of money. Those methods include using multiples such as P/E, estimates of liquidation value, and estimates of replacement costs.

For Questions 1 through 5, answer True or False.

1. The expected long-term rate of consumption growth for the industry's products plus inflation is a good estimate for growth in the continuing value models.

2. The estimate of continuing value after the explicit forecast period cannot be higher than the total value of the firm.

3. Managers are usually overly optimistic about continuing value.

4. In a growing, profitable industry, a company's liquidation value is probably well below the going concern value.

5. The percentage of the firm's value determined by continuing value would most likely increase as the forecast horizon increases.

6. As a firm begins to grow and faces increasing competition as it expands, which of the following is most likely to be the relationships among ROIC on base capital, RONIC, and ROIC on total capital?

A. ROIC on base capital < RONIC < ROIC on total capital.

B. ROIC on base capital > RONIC > ROIC on total capital.

C. ROIC on base capital > ROIC on total capital > RONIC.

D. ROIC on base capital < ROIC on total capital < RONIC.

7. An analyst makes a five-year explicit forecast of revenues of a firm. During those five years, the firm is expected to grow between 10 and 12 percent per year. After that, the growth rate is expected to level off at 8 percent. Should the analyst use a naive base-year extrapolation for the continuing value estimation? Why or why not?

A. No, because it will likely underestimate free cash flow.

B. No, because it will likely overestimate free cash flow.

C. Yes, because it is the most proven method under the given circumstances.

D. Yes, because it is the most proven method in all circumstances.

8. The alternative continuing value measure $CV = (NOPLAT_{t+1})/WACC$ depends on the assumption that:

A. Excess profits will be competed away.

B. WACC is greater than the inflation rate.

C. $NOPLAT_{t+1}$ represents a value from the peak of the business cycle.

D. $NOPLAT_{t+1}$ represents a value from the trough of the business cycle.

9. Which of the following have a positive relationship with economic profit?

I. Growth.

II. RONIC.

III. WACC.

IV. NOPLAT.

A. I and II only.

B. I, II, and IV only.

C. I, III, and IV only.

D. II, III, and IV only.

10. Exhibit 10.9 in the text illustrates how the value of a firm can be broken down into two or more subparts. Which of the following is *not* one of those breakdowns?

A. (1) Nonoperating assets and (2) operating assets plus the present value of the depreciation tax shield.

B. (1) New product line and (2) base business.

C. (1) Present value of continuing value cash flow and (2) the present value of the cash flow from the explicit forecast period.

D. (1) The present value of economic profit from continuing value, (2) the present value of economic profit of the explicit forecast period, and (3) invested capital.

11. List and explain the three non-cash-flow approaches to valuation.

A. _____

B. _____

C. _____

12. If NOPLAT$_{t+1}$ = $200, g = 4%, RONIC = 8%, WACC = 6%, then what is continuing value in year t?

13. An analyst is estimating the continuing value after the explicit forecast period using the economic-profit formula. The analyst estimates that invested capital at the end of the explicit forecast period will be $2,000 and the ROIC on existing capital after the explicit forecast period will be 12 percent. NOPLAT in the year following the explicit forecast period is expected to $500 and is expected to grow at 2 percent per year. The RONIC is expected to be 10 percent, and the cost of capital is 7 percent. What is the continuing value (CV) after the explicit forecast period?

14. Fill in the following table and compute the value of operations.

	Year 1	Year 2	Year 3	CV	Key value drivers	
Revenues	$200.0	$210.0	$216.0	$220.0	Investment rate	60.0%
Operating costs					Return on new capital	15.0%
Operating margin					Growth rate	9.0%
Operating taxes					Operating costs as percent of sales	90.0%
NOPLAT					Operating taxes	30.0%
					NOPLAT margin	7.0%
Net investment						
Free cash flow						
					ROIC	14.0%
Discounted cash flow					Cost of capital	12.0%
Discount rate						
Discounted cash flow						
Value of operations						

11

Estimating the Cost of Capital

The WACC is the opportunity cost of choosing to invest in the business generating the free cash flow (FCF) of that business as opposed to another business of similar risk. For consistency, the estimate of WACC should have the following properties: (1) it includes the opportunity cost of all investors, (2) it uses the appropriate market-based weights, (3) it includes related costs/benefits such as the interest tax shield, (4) it is computed after corporate taxes, (5) it is based on the same expectations of inflation as used in the FCF forecasts, and (6) the duration of the securities used in estimating the WACC equals the duration of the FCFs.

The estimation of WACC requires the estimate of inputs in the following equation:

$$\text{WACC} = \frac{\text{D}}{\text{V}}k_d(1 - T_m) + \frac{\text{E}}{\text{V}}k_e$$

Where D/V is the target weight in debt, E/V is the target weight in equity, k_i is the corresponding required return of each source of capital, and T_m is the marginal tax rate. The capital asset pricing model (CAPM) is a popular way to estimate of the cost of equity:

$$E(R_i) = r_f + \beta_i \times [E(R_m) - r_f]$$

which includes an estimate of the risk-free rate, beta, and the market risk premium. More than one way exists to estimate each of the inputs; there are alternatives to the CAPM such as the Fama-French three-factor model and the arbitrage pricing theory.

The after-tax cost of debt requires an estimate of the required return on debt capital and an estimate of the tax rate. Other estimates include the weights in the target capital structure and, when relevant, the effects of debt equivalents and the effects of a complex capital structure.

1. To estimate the risk-free rate in developed economies, the analyst should use:

    A. Short-term commercial paper.

    B. Short-term government discount instruments.

    C. Long-term coupon-paying government bonds.

    D. Long-term government zero-coupon bonds.

2. In computing the cost of equity for a firm, which of the following are recommended steps in estimating the CAPM beta using regression analysis?

    I. Use a sample size equal to or greater than 60.

    II. Use daily returns.

    III. Use a diversified value-weighted index.

    IV. Watch for possible distortions from market bubbles.

        A. I, II, and III only.

        B. I, III, and IV only.

        C. II and IV only.

        D. II, III, and IV only.

3. The weights to use in the WACC should reflect the:

    A. Current book values.

    B. Current market values.

    C. Target market-based values.

    D. Book values in the case of bonds and market values in the case of equity.

4. Which of the following is *not* an input into the Fama-French three-factor model?

    A. The difference between low book-to-market returns and high book-to-market returns.

    B. The difference between growth stock returns and value stock returns.

    C. The market portfolio returns.

    D. The difference between small-cap returns and large-cap returns.

5. Which of the following are true concerning the index recommended for use in the CAPM?

    I. It should include both traded and untraded investments.

    II. The S&P 500 is the most common proxy for U.S. stocks.

    III. The S&P 500 and the MSCI World index will produce very different results for U.S. stocks.

    IV. For less developed countries, a local market index is recommended.

        A. I and II.

        B. I and IV.

        C. II and III.

        D. III and IV.

6. Bloomberg's recommended adjustment to a firm's beta will:

    A. Lower beta in all cases.

    B. Increase beta in all cases.

    C. Move the beta toward one.

    D. Either increase or decrease beta, but it depends on the size of the standard error of the estimated beta.

7. An analyst uses the past four years of market returns to make a two-year forecast of the market return: $R_{t-3} = 6$ percent, $R_{t-2} = -8$ percent, $R_{t-1} = 0$ percent, and $R_t = 12$ percent. Use the Marshall Blume technique to forecast the annual return for the next two years.

8. An analyst gathers the following information for Firm A and Firm B. Use the information to compute the industry unlevered beta and the appropriate beta for each company for use in the WACC.

Firm A: CAPM beta $= 0.7$; debt-to-equity ratio $= 0.4$

Firm B: CAPM beta $= 1.2$; debt-to-equity ratio $= 2$

9. A firm has a target debt-to-equity ratio of one. Its cost of equity equals 10 percent, the cost of debt is 6 percent, and the tax rate is 40 percent. What is the WACC?

10. A firm has 1,500,000 shares of stock outstanding with a price per share equal to $10. There are 8,000 bonds outstanding, priced at $1,125 each. The cost of equity is 12 percent, the cost of debt is 9 percent, and the corporate tax rate is 34 percent. What is the WACC?

12

Moving from Enterprise Value to Value per Share

Enterprise value is the value of the entire company, which equals the sum of core operations plus nonoperating assets. Subtracting debt, debt equivalents, and hybrid securities, and making other adjustments, provides an estimate of the value of equity. The value of equity divided by undiluted shares outstanding gives value per share. The process should avoid double counting and include valuations of interdependencies between the value of core operations and the value of nonoperating dependencies.

The valuation must carefully evaluate the nonoperating assets, which consist of excess cash and marketable securities, nonconsolidated subsidiaries and equity investments, loans to other companies, finance subsidiaries, discontinued operations, excess real estate, tax loss carry-forwards, and excess pension assets. Debt and debt equivalents consist of debt of all kinds (for example, bonds, bank loans, and commercial paper); operating leases; securitized receivables; unfunded pension liabilities; contingent liabilities; and operating and nonoperating provisions. Hybrid securities consist of convertible debt and convertible preferred stock. Employee stock options and minority interests require additional adjustments.

1. Which of the following is *not* a method for evaluating convertible debt?

   A. Market value.

   B. Multiples valuation.

   C. Black-Scholes valuation.

   D. Conversion price valuation.

2. An analyst is applying an integrated-scenario approach to evaluate operations as well as equity, and the analyst essentially treats equity as a call option on the enterprise value. It is most likely the analysis is of a company that:

    A. Is highly levered.

    B. Has securitized receivables.

    C. Uses income smoothing.

    D. Has excess pension assets or liabilities.

3. In evaluating employee stock options, the exercise value approach provides:

    A. A lower bound of valuation, and using it can undervalue the firm.

    B. An upper bound of valuation, and using it can undervalue the firm.

    C. A lower bound of valuation, and using it can overvalue the firm.

    D. A upper bound of valuation, and using it can overvalue the firm.

4. Company X controls Company Y so that Company Y's financial statements are fully consolidated in the group accounts. With respect to Company X's financial statements, third-party stakes in Company Y:

    A. Are not of concern.

    B. Are to be deducted and are called minority interest.

    C. Are to be added in and are called minority interest.

    D. Are illegal.

5. For equity stakes in subsidiaries where the stake is between 20 and 50 percent of the subsidiary, the holding is recorded on the balance sheet at:

    A. Market value, and the subsidiary's profits are shown below operating profit on the parent company's income statement.

    B. Historical cost plus reinvested income, and the subsidiary's profits are shown in the regular operating profit of the parent company.

    C. Market value, and the subsidiary's profits are shown in the regular operating profit of the parent company.

    D. Historical cost plus reinvested income, and the subsidiary's profits are shown below operating profit on the parent company's income statement.

6. Which of the following correctly lists the conditions when the multiples valuation of a subsidiary is appropriate?

    A. The subsidiary is publicly traded and the parent owns less than 20 percent of the subsidiary.

B. The subsidiary is not publicly traded and the parent owns less than 20 percent of the subsidiary.

C. The subsidiary is publicly traded and the parent owns between 20 percent and 50 percent of the subsidiary.

D. The subsidiary is not publicly traded and the parent owns between 20 percent and 50 percent of the subsidiary.

7. A corporation has 2 million shares outstanding. Using the following information (all value in millions), calculate the value per share.

DCF of operations = $320

Financial subsidiary = $25

Employee stock options = $2

Bonds = $185

Discontinued operations = $2

Securitized receivables = $4

Operating leases = $6

8. Given the following list, put a "+" if it increases a firm's equity value or a "−" if it decreases the firm's value per share of common stock.

Excess real estate	_____
Preferred stock	_____
Minority interest	_____
Tax loss carry-forward	_____
Unfunded pension liabilities	_____
Nonconsolidated subsidiaries	_____

9. Indicate in which cases book value is a reasonable approximation for evaluating the asset or liability. Enter "Yes" if book value is a reasonable approximation and "No" if it is not.

A. Floating-rate debt: _____

B. Outstanding bonds that are secure and actively traded: _____

C. Discontinued operations: _____

D. Stake in a publicly traded subsidiary: _____

    E. Excess real estate: _____

    F. Loans to nonconsolidated subsidiaries and
other companies (assume interest rates and
credit risk have not changed): _____

    G. An outstanding convertible bond deep
in the money: _____

    H. Employee stock options: _____

10. An analyst is evaluating a corporation's subsidiary by multiplying the value of the stake in the subsidiary when it was acquired times 1 plus the percentage change in a portfolio of comparable stocks over the same holding period. Based on this information, answer the following questions:

    A. What are the conditions when this is a preferred method of valuation for the stake?

    B. What is the name of the method?

13

Calculating and Interpreting Results

After getting comfortable with the workings of a model, an analyst should use scenario analysis to deepen the understanding offered by the valuations. In the case of a company that consists of multiple business units, the analyst should use a sum-of-the-parts valuation.

Verifying valuation results involves checks and balances to see if the model is technically robust by addressing the following relationships: (1) that the balance sheet balances and the correct relationships exist among income, retained earnings, and dividends; (2) that the sum of invested capital plus nonoperating assets equals the cumulative sources of financing; and (3) that the change in excess cash and debt line up with the cash flow statement. A good model will have automatic checks for these relationships.

Checking for economic consistency involves seeing if the results reflect appropriate value driver economics; for example, high growth and return should be reflected in value of operations higher than book value. The analyst should also check to see if the patterns of key financial and operating ratios are consistent with economic logic and, in general, check to see if the results are plausible.

Sensitivity analysis aids in determining the impact of changes of key drivers, and scenario analysis allows for assessing results under a broad set of conditions. Valuation can be very sensitive to small changes in assumptions, which is why market values fluctuate. A good guide is to aim for a valuation range of +/−15 percent, which is similar to the range used by investment bankers.

1. Which of the following are issues in the creation of the financial statements for business units?

   I. Allocating corporate overhead costs.

   II. Dealing with intercompany transactions.

   III. Estimating unit betas.

   IV. Dealing with incomplete information when using public information.

      A. I and II only.

      B. II and IV only.

      C. I, II, and IV only.

      D. II, III, and IV only.

2. Which of the following is *not* a question related to economic consistency of a model?

   A. Are the patterns intended?

   B. Are the patterns reasonable?

   C. Are the patterns chartable?

   D. Are the patterns consistent with industry dynamics?

3. To prioritize strategic actions, the analyst should:

   A. Take a vote from the major players.

   B. Build a sensitivity analysis that tests multiple changes at a time.

   C. Follow the priorities of leaders in the industry.

   D. Follow Porter's five points.

4. For multibusiness units, consolidated corporate results:

   A. Must eliminate internal revenues, costs, and profits.

   B. Are not possible.

   C. Are computed by summing the inputs for each accounting entry across units.

   D. Are computed by top-down algorithms that give estimated values based on the economic profit or cost of each entry.

5. Which of the following correctly describes how to determine the beta for a business unit within a multiple-business corporation?

   A. Use the average of the equity betas for the industry.

   B. Use the beta of the multi-unit enterprise.

   C. Relever the unlevered sector median beta using the capital structure of the unit.

   D. Relever the unlevered sector median beta using the capital structure of the entire multiple-business corporation.

6. List the criteria for assessing whether a model is technically robust with respect to the following three perspectives.

   A. Unadjusted financial statements: _____

   B. Rearranged financial statements: _____

   C. Statement of cash flows: _____

7. When analyzing scenarios in a scenario analysis, an analyst should review the assumptions of a model with respect to four variables. List and explain those variables.

   A. _____

   B. _____

   C. _____

   D. _____

8. When making forecasts, increasing one variable usually means decreasing another. List three of the several possible common trade-offs that should be considered in making such forecasts.

   A. _____

   B. _____

   C. _____

9. An analyst is estimating the ROIC of a company that has zero fixed costs per unit and pays no taxes. The analyst makes the following forecasts. Sales next year will equal 200 units and will increase at 10 percent for each of the two following years. Prices per unit will be $100, $104, and $110, which simply embody inflation forecasts. Costs per unit will be constant. Current capital invested is $2,000, and the firm will reinvest 50 percent of income.

   What will be the ROIC for each of the three years?

	Year 1	Year 2	Year 3
Number of units			
Price per unit			
Cost per unit			
Income			
Invested capital			
ROIC			

If this is a competitive industry, are the results realistic? Why or why not?

10. The forecasts in Question 9 used several assumptions. Repeat the forecasts where A) costs increase with inflation, but all other assumptions hold, and B) sales remain constant, but all the other assumptions hold (including constant costs).

A.

	Year 1	Year 2	Year 3
Number of units			
Price per unit			
Cost per unit			
Income			
Invested capital			
ROIC			

B.

	Year 1	Year 2	Year 3
Number of units			
Price per unit			
Cost per unit			
Income			
Invested capital			
ROIC			

11. Based on the results in Question 10, assess the sensitivity of your results in Question 9 to each of the relaxed assumptions.

14

Using Multiples to Triangulate Results

The use of multiples can increase valuations based on DCF analysis. There are three requirements for making useful analyses of comparable multiples: (1) use the right multiple, (2) calculate the multiple in a consistent manner, and (3) use the right peer group. The right multiple is often the value-to-EBITA ratio:

$$\frac{\text{Value}}{\text{EBITA}} = \frac{(1 - T)\left(1 - \frac{g}{\text{ROIC}}\right)}{\text{WACC} - g}$$

This measure is superior to the price-to-earnings (P/E) ratio because (1) capital structure affects P/E, and (2) nonoperating gains and losses affect earnings. Alternatives to the value-to-EBITA multiple include the value-to-revenue ratio and the price-to-earnings-growth (PEG) ratio. This measure and other multiples should be forward-looking rather than based on historical data.

Ratios should be calculated in a consistent manner. In the case of the value-to-EBITA multiple, one important step is to include in the ratio all investor capital attributable to assets that generate EBITA. Finally, the peer group is important. The peer group should consist of companies whose underlying characteristics (such as production methodology, distribution channels, and R&D) lead to similar growth and ROIC characteristics.

1. Which two of the following are likely to vary the most among companies within an industry?

   I. Tax rates.

   II. Growth.

   III. ROIC.

   IV. WACC.

     A. I and II.

     B. I and III.

     C. II and III.

     D. III and IV.

2. Which of the following are reasons that the value-to-EBITA ratio is superior to the price-to-earnings ratio as a multiple to aid in valuation?

   I. The P/E is distorted by capital structure.

   II. The P/E is distorted by inflation.

   III. The P/E is distorted by nonoperating gains and losses.

   IV. The P/E is distorted by dividend payouts.

     A. I and III only.

     B. II and III only.

     C. II and IV only.

     D. I, III, and IV only.

3. Comparison of a company's multiples to the arithmetic averages of an industry:

     A. Is one of the more recommended practices, but it may not be the best.

     B. Is the best recommended practice.

     C. Is not recommended.

     D. Is not possible.

4. Increasing growth and ROIC by the same amount and holding taxes and WACC constant will:

     A. Increase the value-to-EBITA ratio.

     B. Not affect the value-to-EBITA ratio.

     C. Decrease the value-to-EBITA ratio.

     D. Have an undetermined effect on the value-to-EBITA ratio.

5. Given that the value-to-EBITA ratio of a company is 4.5 and the projected EBITA growth rate is 3 percent, what is the adjusted PEG ratio?

6. Given the following inputs, compute the value-to-EBITA ratio: Tax rate = 34 percent, growth rate = 4 percent, ROIC = 10 percent, and WACC = 9 percent.

7. An all-equity firm has $200 in cash and $800 in fixed assets that will never need to be replaced. The interest earned on cash is 2 percent. The revenues are $150 and are expected to grow at 5 percent. The tax rate is 40 percent, and the WACC is 10 percent. What is the value-to-EBITA ratio based on operations?

8. For each of the following characteristics that help determine growth and ROIC, list contrasting types of the characteristics to consider when composing appropriate peer groups.
   A. Production methodology: _____
   B. Distribution channels: _____
   C. Research and development: _____

9. Explain why EBITA is superior to:
   A. EBIT: _____
   _____
   B. EBITDA: _____
   _____

10. Give examples of nonfinancial ratios applied to Internet companies in the 1990s. Comment on their relative usefulness in the valuation of Internet stocks before such stocks matured and the valuation of Internet stocks after the industry matured.

15

Market Value Tracks Return on Invested Capital and Growth

Despite wide swings in prices over the years, the market data shows that individual stocks and the market as a whole follow fundamental laws; for example, return on capital and growth are the main drivers of company values in capital markets. The median price-to-earnings ratio has hovered around 15 over the long term. In the following formula, the reinvestment ratio equals growth divided by return on equity (g/ROE), which has been about 0.5 over time. Using an estimate of 3.167 percent for the average growth rate gives an expected return equal to 6.5 percent:

$$\text{Expected return} = \frac{E}{P} \times \left(1 - \frac{g}{\text{ROE}}\right) + g = \frac{1}{15} \times (1 - 0.5) + 0.03167 = 0.065$$

Actual returns have varied across the five recent economic eras: the carefree Sixties (1960–1968), the great inflation (1968–1982), the return to normalcy (1982–1996), the technology bubble (1996–2004), and the leveraging and credit crisis (2004–2008). In each period, the returns have closely tracked changes in fundamental values.

Total return to shareholders (TRS) is measured by changes in the market valuation and driven not only by changes in the key drivers but also by changes in investor expectations, which are more important in the short run. TRS can be low for firms with high ROIC and growth if investors already have expectations for the high ROIC and growth. Also, price-to-earnings multiples do not necessarily reflect the differences in the key drivers, and two companies with very different ROICs can have similar earnings multiples.

1. Which of the following are properties that should lead to firms having higher value in the stock market?

   I. Higher P/E.

  II. First-in first-out (FIFO) accounting.

 III. Higher growth.

 IV. ROIC greater than the cost of capital.

    A. I and II only.

    B. I, II, and III only.

    C. III and IV only.

    D. II, III, and IV only.

2. The relationship between total return to shareholders and the drivers ROIC and growth:

    A. Is not strong at all.

    B. Is strong, and stronger over the short term than the long term.

    C. Is strong, and stronger over the long term than the short term.

    D. Is strong, and equally strong over the short term and the long term.

3. Which two of the following situations will create the most value?

   I. A high-ROIC company increasing P/E.

  II. A high-growth company increasing P/E.

 III. A high-ROIC company increasing growth.

 IV. A high-growth company increasing ROIC.

    A. I and II only.

    B. I and III only.

    C. II and III only.

    D. III and IV only.

4. Over the past 200 years, equities have, on average, achieved total returns to shareholders equal to about:

    A. 4.5 percent.

    B. 5.0 percent.

    C. 6.5 percent.

    D. 8.0 percent.

5. For companies with constant growth and return on capital, P/E is defined as:

   A. $(ROE)/(k-g)$.

   B. $(1-g/ROE)/(k-g)$.

   C. $(ROE)/(ROE-g)$.

   D. $[(1/ROE)-1]/(k-g)$.

6. According to Exhibit 15.5 in the text, which is true of the two sectors with the highest and next to highest market-value/capital ratio?

   I. Their market-value/earnings ratios were the highest and next to highest, respectively.

   II. Their ROICs were the highest and next to highest, respectively.

   III. Their growth rates were the highest and next to highest, respectively.

   IV. Their P/E ratios were the highest and next to highest, respectively.

     A. I and II only.

     B. I and IV only.

     C. I, II, and III only.

     D. II, III, and IV only.

7. Regression results are reported in Exhibit 15.7 in the text. There are results of two regressions where the sample size was over 2,000 companies. One regression was that of market-value/earnings on ROIC and growth. The other regression was that of market-value/capital on ROIC and growth. Which of the following is most accurate concerning the results?

   A. The R-squared values for both of these regressions were near zero and not significant.

   B. The R-squared value for market-value/earnings was near zero and that for market-value/capital was over 50 percent.

   C. The R-squared value for market-value/capital was near zero and that for market-value/earnings was over 50 percent.

   D. The R-squared values for both of these regressions were between 20 and 40 percent.

8. Total return to shareholders (TRS) is:

   A. Increasingly correlated with ROIC as growth rises.

   B. Increasingly correlated with growth as ROIC rises.

   C. Not correlated with either ROIC or growth over the long run.

   D. Less correlated with ROIC as growth rises.

9. Match the description of market conditions on the right with the corresponding time period on the left by putting the appropriate letter in the blank.

1960–1968: _____   A. TRS averaged 5 percent and was very volatile.

1968–1982: _____   B. Interest rates and inflation fell, and TRS was more than 16 percent.

1982–1996: _____

1996–2004: _____   C. TRS averaged –5 percent per year and was very volatile.

2004–2008: _____   D. There was low inflation and an average TRS per year of 9 percent.

                        E. Inflation increased and TRS averaged –1 percent per year.

10. Given the following inputs, compute the expected return: Growth = 5 percent, P/E = 20, and ROE = 25 percent.

16

Markets Value Substance, Not Form

Return on invested capital (ROIC) and growth are the only drivers of value creation, yet managers often spend time and resources attempting to smooth earnings, meet earnings targets, stay listed in a stock index, and become cross-listed. The evidence shows that the stock market does not reward these efforts, nor do changes in accounting rules and stock splits have lasting effects. These issues do not have an effect on stock returns unless they reflect a change in fundamental value.

Firms that have a good record of beating earnings forecasts tend to have more favorable stock returns; however, this record is usually the result of the favorable earnings reflecting a positive fundamental change and not just that earnings were higher than the forecast. Thus, managers should not focus too much on meeting earnings expectations; in fact, the efforts of managers to pursue these goals may have detrimental effects on the firm (e.g., lowering advertising expenditures to increase revenue in a given period).

Listing and delisting from an index do not seem to have long-term effects for any given firm. Although there can be a negative effect initially from delisting, the effect usually reverses in a few months. Furthermore, cross-listing within developed markets does not have an effect; however, firms in emerging markets may benefit from cross-listing in a developed market.

Investors apparently see through accounting changes. If investors focused on earnings, for example, a move from FIFO to LIFO would lower the share price, but it generally does the opposite because of the increase in cash flows.

As another example, mere changes in goodwill do not affect share price; however, a change in goodwill that is associated with a real change in the firm produces a reaction from sophisticated investors.

1. Reactions of investors to earnings surprises:
   A. Have not been studied long enough for researchers to reach conclusions.
   B. Have been found to be rational when the surprise indicated a real change in the fundamentals of the firm.
   C. Have been studied for a long time and there are some patterns, but the reasons are still a mystery.
   D. Justify the attention that managers pay to meeting earnings targets.

2. The point of Exhibit 16.2 in the text is to show:
   A. That even the companies with the lowest earnings volatility do not have smooth earnings.
   B. The negative relationship between earnings volatility and returns to shareholders.
   C. The positive relationship between earnings volatility and returns to shareholders.
   D. The significant change in stock returns that occurs when the managers of a company engage in earnings smoothing.

3. Academic research has found that share prices of companies that are removed from a major stock index:
   A. Trend down until significant news arrives to reverse the trend.
   B. Do not experience any abnormal returns either in the short term or in the long term.
   C. Drop immediately and then begin trading normally.
   D. Drop immediately, but the decline is usually reversed within one or two months.

4. Which of the following are valid reasons that cross-listing might actually improve a company's stock performance?
   I. Improved corporate governance.
   II. Trading in multiple time zones.
   III. Access to an increased number of investors.
   IV. Affirmation effect of being listed in more than one developed market.
      A. I, II, and IV only.
      B. I and III only.

C. II and III only.

D. II, III, and IV only.

5. Which of the following are valid reasons that a firm's stock split can be followed by an increase in the value of the shares of that firm?

I. Signaling.

II. Liquidity.

III. Fiat effect.

IV. Self-selection.

    A. I and IV only.

    B. II and III only.

    C. II, III, and IV only.

    D. None of these.

6. According to the evidence concerning moving to/from LIFO from/to FIFO as illustrated in Exhibit 16.9 in the text, which of the following is most accurate?

A. The stocks of firms switching to LIFO experience positive returns, but those switching from LIFO do not show any change in returns.

B. The stocks of firms switching to LIFO experience positive returns, and those switching from LIFO experience negative returns.

C. The stocks of firms switching to LIFO do not show any change in returns, and neither do the stocks of firms switching from LIFO.

D. The stocks of firms switching from LIFO experience positive returns, and those switching to LIFO experience negative returns.

7. Voluntary option expensing has been found to have which of the following?

A. A negative impact on share price.

B. A positive impact on share price.

C. No impact on share price.

D. A positive impact if LIFO accounting is used and a negative effect if FIFO accounting is used.

8. An analysis of 50 European companies that began reporting using U.S. GAAP over the period 1997 to 2004 found which of the following?

I. Earnings under GAAP were generally lower than earnings under the home country's rules.

II. The differences in earnings under the two regimes were all less than 10 percent.

III. The stocks of the 50 companies generally reacted positively when the disclosures were made.

IV. Executives had concerns over the impact of reporting under U.S. GAAP.

    A. I and II only.

    B. I, II, and III only.

    C. I, III, and IV only.

    D. II, III, and IV only.

9. The effect of goodwill amortization on share prices has been found to be:

    A. Positive and significant overall.

    B. Negative and significant overall.

    C. Significantly positive or negative depending on whether FIFO or LIFO is used.

    D. Of little importance.

10. Which of the following is true concerning information in Exhibit 16.4 in the text?

    A. The market reactions to announcements of development successes were all positive and the reactions to development setbacks were all negative, and the negative values were generally larger than the positive ones in absolute value terms.

    B. The market reactions to announcements of development successes were all positive and the reactions to development setbacks were all negative, and the positive values were generally larger than the negative ones in absolute value terms.

    C. The market reactions to announcements of development successes were mostly, but not all, positive and the reactions to development setbacks were all negative, and the positive values were equal to the negative ones in absolute value terms.

    D. Although there is evidence that announcements of setbacks and successes have an impact on returns, it is not significantly different from zero, indicating that individual success and setbacks are secondary to fundamentals.

11. List the three ways the managers of firms may try to meet earnings forecasts and the effect they may have on share price.

    A. _____

    B. _____

    C. _____

17

Emotions and Mispricing
in the Market

Behavioral finance posits three conditions that can lead to market mispricings: (1) when individual investors behave irrationally, (2) when systematic patterns of irrational behavior emerge among investors, and (3) when there are limits to arbitrage in financial markets. Individual company deviations from fundamental values are rare, and market deviations are even rarer. Both deviations correct themselves quickly unless there is a market barrier that limits arbitrage (e.g., short-selling constraints or a small float in the case of an individual stock). Noise-trader risk also produces temporary anomalies.

Two possible sources of mispricings are: (1) the combinations of overreaction, underreaction, reversal, and momentum, and (2) bubbles and bursts. Mispricing can occur if investors place too much weight on recent information, but the evidence is mixed on whether this can happen to a significant degree, or if it can happen to an extent that trading on the mispricing produces profit after subtracting transaction costs. Bubbles have occurred, but they are rare. Unrealistic expectations of continued growth, which led to excessively high P/E ratios, caused the tech bubble in the late 1990s. High earnings that were not sustainable caused the credit bubble a decade later. Thus, in the latter case, it was not that the P/E ratios were too high, but that the earnings in the ratio eventually had to fall.

For Questions 1 through 10, answer True or False.

1. Market-wide price deviations usually are corrected within one year.

2. Random deviations from intrinsic value can occur in stock prices, but managers are best off assuming that the market will correctly reflect the intrinsic value of their decisions.

3. One barrier to correcting mispricing is a small free float.

4. Academics agree that short-term momentum and reversal patterns in stock prices are driven by placing too much weight on the most recent information.

5. Both the 2000 bubble and the 2007 bubble were valuation bubbles.

6. The P/E ratios in 2007 were greater than the P/E ratios in 2000.

7. From the 1970s to 2000, the expansion of credit markets grew hand in hand with economic growth.

8. Behavioral finance theorists propose that large groups of investors can start showing the same nonrational patterns of investment behavior at the same time, which can lead to persistent price deviations.

9. Market-wide price deviations from fair value are less frequent than individual company share price deviations from the company's fundamental value.

10. Behavioral finance cannot yet explain why investors overreact in the case of initial public offerings (IPOs) and underreact with respect to earnings announcements.

11. In the 1999 stock bubble, most of the large-capitalization companies with high P/Es were clustered in all of the following sectors *except*:
    A. Utilities.
    B. Technology.
    C. Media.
    D. Telecommunications.

12. Noise-trader risk is defined as:
    A. A market barrier that contributes to sharp reversals.
    B. A market barrier that prevents corrections from overpricing.
    C. An input into the Fama-French three-factor model measured by the residual of the CAPM.
    D. One of the unproven theories of the proponents of behavioral finance.

13. Which of the following was *not* one of the faster growing sectors in the period 2000–2006?

   A. The energy sector.

   B. The financial sector.

   C. The transportation sector.

   D. The utilities sector.

14. Before its collapse in 1998, Long-Term Capital Management (LTCM) had taken a large long position in Shell and a large short position in Royal Dutch. Which of the following is most accurate concerning the results of these positions?

   A. The positions were based on erroneous valuations based on a bubble theory, and both stocks continued to increase. Unfortunately for LTCM, Royal Dutch increased more than Shell, and the subsequent losses helped contribute to LTCM's decline.

   B. The positions were based on correct valuations, and the profits earned help mitigate the losses in other areas (e.g., those caused by the default of Russia).

   C. The positions were based on correct valuations, but market turmoil led to huge losses in the positions before profits could be realized from a return to fundamental valuations.

   D. The positions were based on erroneous valuations based on a momentum theory, and when the reversals did not occur, LTCM experienced huge losses that contributed to its decline.

15. Which of the following statements are true concerning the growth of Asian economies since 2000?

   I. The growth has boosted demand for commodities.

   II. India and China have been large emerging economies.

   III. The growth is largely seen as an unsustainable bubble.

   IV. The growth is causing a savings deficit in the region.

   A. I and II only.

   B. I, II, and IV only.

   C. II, III, and IV only.

   D. II and IV only.

16. Explain network effects and how incorrectly applying the concept contributed to one of the stock market bubbles.

18

Investors and Managers in Efficient Markets

There are many types of investors, ranging from rational to much less rational, but markets can be efficient even when all investors are not rational. Thus, managers of firms should still focus on the key drivers and not concern themselves with cosmetic measures associated with entries such as goodwill, nor with activities like the smoothing of quarterly earnings. There is a benefit, however, in understanding their investor base.

Prices can be volatile because a small percentage error in an important input can lead to a percent deviation many times larger in the price. The evidence suggests that markets are efficient enough to provide meaningful signals about the cost of capital for investment decisions because prices will generally be within a +/−20 percent bandwidth around intrinsic value at any point in time. The wide swings can occur as informed investors react to a realized under- or overpricing of the stock or new information. As the informed investors begin to buy or sell, noise traders begin following their actions to the point of mispricing in the other extreme, which then starts the cycle over again. Trading by informed investors sets upper and lower bounds around the intrinsic values, but with more uncertainty the bounds are wider. Furthermore, extreme volatility can exist within the bounds, but prices outside of the bounds occur only in rare circumstances such as when noise traders outnumber informed investors.

Retail investors make up about 40 percent of the U.S. equity investors, but they do not move prices much. Institutional investors can be broken down into three categories: intrinsic investors, traders, and mechanical investors. With respect to the institutional investor market, they make up 20 to 25 percent,

35 to 40 percent, and 35 to 40 percent, respectively. Although traders do the majority of trading in a year, the intrinsic investors' activities have the largest impact on share prices. This level of impact implies that managers should focus on creating intrinsic value.

1. Which of the following is/are correct concerning how managers should perceive short-term volatility of their stock?

   I. See it as a sign of market inefficiency.

   II. Take it into account when driving ROIC.

   III. Take it into account when driving growth.

   IV. Note that it will be higher when there is more uncertainty.

   A. I, II, and III only.

   B. I and IV only.

   C. II and III only.

   D. IV only.

2. According to Exhibit 18.1 in the text, which is a graph of the theoretical price changes of a stock, the difference between the upper trading boundary and lower trading boundary:

   A. Is less than the difference between the upper intrinsic value and the lower intrinsic value.

   B. Is equal to the difference between the upper intrinsic value and the lower intrinsic value.

   C. Is greater than the difference between the upper intrinsic value and the lower intrinsic value.

   D. Has no set relationship to the upper intrinsic value and the lower intrinsic value.

3. The prototypical mechanical investor would best be described as a/an:

   A. Index fund.

   B. Hedge fund.

   C. Growth mutual fund.

   D. Value mutual fund.

4. The title of "informed trader" would most aptly apply to:

   A. Intrinsic investors.

   B. Traders.

   C. Quants.

   D. Closet indexers.

5. Which of the following characterize noise traders?
   I. They do not care about intrinsic value.
   II. They are always in the minority.
   III. They can move price outside the bounds of intrinsic value.
   IV. They trade on small events.
      A. I and II only.
      B. I, III, and IV only.
      C. II, III, and IV only.
      D. II and IV only.

6. Which of the following are true of retail investors?
   I. They are major contributors to stock volatility within the bounds set by intrinsic investors.
   II. Their opinions should not be a major concern of managers.
   III. They trade a great deal.
   IV. They make up about 40 percent of U.S. equity investors.
      A. I and III only.
      B. I, III, and IV only.
      C. II, III, and IV only.
      D. II and IV only.

7. Which of the following are recommended when corporate managers perceive that market prices or multiples are high for their businesses or segments within a multi-unit company?
   I. Issue additional shares.
   II. Pay for an acquisition with company shares instead of cash.
   III. Split the stock.
   IV. Divest business segments.
      A. I and III only.
      B. I, II, and IV only.
      C. II, III, and IV only.
      D. None of these.

8. The following table lists the institutional investor segments in the left column. The remaining columns indicate types of activity. In each column, place an H for highest, M for median, or L for lowest to indicate whether the associated type of investor is the highest, the median, or the lowest for the activity indicated in the heading.

Type of investor	Number of positions	Total trading per year per investment	Effective trading per day	Total trading per year per segment
Intrinsic				
Trader				
Mechanical				

9. Match the type of investor on the left with the investor definition on the right.

Intrinsic: _____

Trader: _____

Mechanical: _____

A. Seeks profits by betting on short-term movements.

B. Makes decisions based on strict criteria.

C. Scrutinizes investments for a month or more before taking positions.

10. Explain the reason that managers need to understand their investor base.

19

Corporate Portfolio Strategy

Each firm should manage its portfolio of businesses by determining whether it is the best owner of each business in the portfolio (i.e., whether it can create the most value from each business it owns). If so, then the firm should keep the business. If not, the firm should divest the business for a value that exceeds its value to the firm. It should use the same basic philosophy when considering adding businesses to the portfolio.

Firms that can add the most value to a business usually have one of five advantages: (1) unique links with other businesses within the firm, (2) distinctive skills, (3) better governance, (4) better insight and foresight, and (5) an influence on critical stakeholders. The firm that can offer one or more of these advantages can change over time as the firm, business, or economy changes. At the beginning of a business, for example, the founders are the best managers, but this will usually change. The needs of the business change as it expands and needs additional capital, a wider variety of management skills, and more connections to other businesses such as buyers and suppliers. A typical path of a business begins with the founders and ends in a conglomerate corporation.

When constructing a portfolio of businesses, the firm should take five steps: (1) assess the firm's current value, (2) identify internal opportunities to improve operations, (3) determine if some businesses in the firm should be divested, (4) identify potential acquisitions or other initiatives to create new growth, and (5) assess if the company's value can increase from changes in capital structure. Diversification considerations are not part of the list. There is no evidence to support the idea that diversification increases value or that investors are willing to pay more for a diversified firm. Diversification can hurt the value of the firm, however, if it lowers the ability of the managers to focus on how to create value for each of the multifarious businesses.

1. List and explain the five main reasons a given firm might be the best owner of a business.

    A. _____

    B. _____

    C. _____

    D. _____

    E. _____

2. From the list of potential owners, choose which is most likely to be the best owner given the indicated need in the list that follows. Put the appropriate letter in the blank. Some are used more than once. In most cases, there is one best answer, but others might apply.

    A. Private equity.

    B. Founders.

    C. Conglomerate.

    D. Venture capital.

       i. Managerial experience: _____

       ii. Distribution channels: _____

       iii. Additional funds: _____

       iv. Dynamic decision making: _____

       v. Innovation: _____

       vi. Supplier network: _____

       vii. Recapitalization: _____

3. Given the list to the right, match each activity to its corresponding level in the five-step value-adding process from lowest to highest on the left. One activity does not belong on the list.

i. _____	A. Consider a trade sale of a business.
ii. _____	B. Determine the optimal capital structure.
iii. _____	C. Determine diversification effects.
iv. _____	D. Assess the gaps between the valuations of owners and managers.
v. _____	E. Identify growth initiatives.
	F. Identify possible improvements of margins and efficiency.

4. Read the case and then answer the questions that follow.

   Conglom Corporation owns three businesses: CleanUp, Ennerall, and Corwin Company. CleanUp makes and distributes soap and shampoo. Ennerall developed a new vitamin-rich energy drink three years ago with a newly discovered extract from a jungle herb. The sales of the drink rose dramatically when it was first introduced to the market. Corwin Company makes razor blades. CleanUp is the core business of Conglom Corporation and generates 70 percent of the discounted cash flows. It has a low cost of capital, and its ROIC is above the cost of capital. It acquired Ennerall when its contacts in the convenience store industry got samples of Ennerall's product, which quickly sold. After two years of quick growth via CleanUp's drugstore connections, the uniqueness of Ennerall's product has worn off, and sales have leveled off. The managers of Ennerall have been investing large sums attempting to develop new variations of their product that they hope will steal market share from their rivals. Corwin Company was a family business that had lost a lot of value due to the heirs of the founders neglecting the business and not monitoring the managers. Conglom bought the Corwin Company because the price was attractive, and the sales and marketing team of CleanUp helped increase the value of the Corwin Company to the point where its returns and growth are on par with CleanUp's.

   A. In the case of Ennerall and Corwin Company, indicate what likely made Conglom the best owner in each case. Mention at least one of the five reasons a given firm might be the best owner as listed in the text.

      Ennerall: _____

      Corwin Company: _____

   B. Should Conglom divest either Ennerall or Corwin Company? Why?

20

Performance Management

Performance management systems align decisions with short- and long-term objectives and the overall strategy. Such systems typically include long-term strategic plans, short-term budgets, capital budgeting systems, performance reporting and reviews, and compensation frameworks. The rigor and honesty of implementing the system is at least as important as the system itself. Implementing the system includes choosing the metrics, composing the scorecard, and setting the meeting calendars.

Choosing the right metrics means identifying the value drivers. Typically, the ultimate drivers are long-term growth, ROIC, and the cost of capital. Short-term, medium-term, and long-term value drivers determine growth, ROIC, and the cost of capital. Short-term value drivers are usually the easiest to quantify, and examples include sales productivity, operating cost productivity, and capital productivity. Medium-term value drivers consist of measures of commercial health, cost structure health, and asset health. Long-term value drivers address strategic issues such as ways to exploit new growth areas and the existence of potential market threats. Understanding the value drivers allows the managers to have a common language for their goals and to make better choices of trade-offs between critical and less critical drivers.

Managers should follow some of the guidelines of the balanced score-card approach, introduced by Robert S. Kaplan and David P. Norton in "The Balanced Scorecard: Measures That Drive Performance" (*Harvard Business Review*, February 1992), which can reflect many aspects of the firm and its goals. However, the choice of critical drivers should be tailored to the firm's businesses. For example, in contrast to the balanced scorecard approach, a tree based on profit-and-loss structure is often the most natural and easiest to complete. The targets need to be challenging and realistic, and should not consist of only a single point. One recommendation is the use of base and stretch targets, where achieving the latter reaps a reward for the manager and not a penalty.

In addition to determining drivers and targets, managers should assess organizational health, which is determined by the people, skills, and culture of the company. Managers should help set the targets to better understand these issues. Fact-based reviews with appropriate rewards should depend on: (1) stock performance where macroeconomic and industry trends have been removed, (2) long-term assessments that might mean deferring rewards, and (3) measures of performance against both quantitative and qualitative drivers. The firm should harness the power of nonfinancial incentives, such as creating a culture that attracts and motivates quality employees.

1. Assessing the ability to exploit new growth areas and potential new threats is the focus of:

   A. Short-term value drivers.

   B. Medium-term value drivers.

   C. Long-term value drivers.

   D. None of these.

2. Which of the following are components of a good planning and performance management system?

   I. Promoting a common language of goals and performance.

   II. Including metrics, corporate meeting calendars, and scorecards.

   III. Promoting an understanding of value drivers.

   IV. Having honesty and rigor in implementation.

      A. I, II, and III only.

      B. I, III, and IV only.

      C. II, III, and IV only.

      D. I, II, III, and IV.

3. Which of the following are true of the balanced scorecard method introduced by Kaplan and Norton (1992)?

   I. It posits that there are more measures of performance than just financial performance.

   II. It is used by both profit and nonprofit organizations.

   III. It advocates that companies choose their own set of metrics for the outermost branches of the value creation tree.

   IV. Customer satisfaction and learning are as important as long-term value creation.

      A. I and II only.

      B. I, II, and III only.

C. I, II, and IV only.

D. II, III, and IV only.

4. What is the role of the operating managers in setting the targets and in reading the measures they are targeting?

A. None.

B. Operating managers should set targets but should not be involved in reading the measures.

C. Operating managers should be involved in reading the measures but not in setting the targets.

D. Operating managers should be involved in both setting the targets and reading the measures.

5. The recommendation concerning stock-based compensation is:

A. Not to use it at all.

B. That it has been proven to be the best method to motivate managers because markets are efficient.

C. It is useful, but macroeconomic and industry effects should be removed in formulating the compensation.

D. It should be used sporadically depending on the conditions of the market.

6. Commercial health metrics indicate whether the company can do what with its current revenue growth?

7. What is one key issue concerning accurately assessing a company's recent strong growth relative to long-term growth?

8. A well-defined and appropriately selected set of key value drivers ought to allow management to do what?

9. A diagnostic check of organizational health would typically measure what four aspects of the firm?

A. _____

B. _____

C. _____

D. _____

10. Indicate whether each of the following value drivers is a short-term driver, a medium-term driver, or a long-term driver.

A. Asset health: _____

B. Operating cost productivity: _____

C. Cost structure health: _____

D. Strategic health: _____

E. Sales productivity: _____

F. Capital productivity: _____

G. Commercial health: _____

11. Explain an alternative to a single-point performance target that uses two points of reference, how those points are determined, and how managers should be motivated with respect to them.

21

Mergers and Acquisitions

Acquisitions rarely create value unless they do one or more of the following: (1) improve performance of the target company, (2) remove excess capacity, (3) create market access for the acquirer's or target's products, (4) acquire skills or technologies at a lower cost and/or more quickly than could be done without the acquisition, and (5) pick winners early. Most of the value of an acquisition goes to the target's shareholders unless one or more of the following hold for the acquirer: (1) it had strong performance before the acquisition, (2) it can pay a low premium, and (3) it had fewer competitors in the bidding process. The value created for the acquirer is:

Value Created for Acquirer = (Stand-Alone Value of Target

+ Value of Performance Improvements)

− (Market Value of Target + Acquisition Premium)

Empirical research has shown that acquisitions have come in waves and generally rose when stock prices were high, interest rates were low, and one or more large deals had already taken place. Also, only about a third of the deals created value for the acquirer, a third destroyed value, and the remaining third had unclear results.

Cost savings can create value, but estimating those savings requires a framework. As an example for a generic firm, the analyst might allocate the savings into six categories: R&D, procurement, manufacturing, sales and marketing, distribution, and administration. Assumed cost savings should be estimated and categorized in detail to avoid double counting. It is recommended that those directly involved in the cost-savings process be involved in the estimations of cost savings.

Revenue analysis has both explicit and implicit considerations. Revenue improvements generally have four sources: (1) increasing sales to a higher peak level, (2) reaching a peak level faster, (3) extending the life of products, and (4) adding new products. Usually revenue does not increase unless prices can rise, but antitrust regulation can prevent higher prices unless the quality of the products increases.

Generally, an acquiring firm's stockholders benefit more if the firm uses stock instead of cash for the acquisition. Although the stock offering can lead to dilution, it lowers the risk to the acquirer and allocates more risk to the target firm's shareholders. Research has shown that stock prices react to creation of intrinsic value in an acquisition and that dilution and other accounting issues do not matter.

1. Which of the following correctly summarizes the approximate proportion of acquisitions that create or destroy value for the acquiring company's shareholders?

    A. Approximately 20 percent create value, 20 percent destroy value, and for the remaining it is not clear.

    B. Approximately $33\frac{1}{3}$ percent create value, $33\frac{1}{3}$ percent destroy value, and for the remaining it is not clear.

    C. Approximately 50 percent create value, 20 percent destroy value, and for the remaining it is not clear.

    D. Approximately 66 percent create value, 17 percent destroy value, and for the remaining it is not clear.

2. Which of the following has been found to be a predictor concerning whether an acquiring firm's shareholders will benefit from an acquisition?

    A. The size of the target.

    B. The P/E of the acquirer is higher than that of the target before the acquisition.

    C. The target and the acquirer are in the same industry.

    D. The acquirer had strong earnings and price growth for several years before the acquisition.

3. The analysis of cost savings should include an industry-specific business system. Which of the following is *not* one of the three criteria that an insightful business system will fulfill?

    A. Uses a top-down approach.

    B. Assigns each cost item of the target to one segment of the business system.

    C. Uses detail to identify the precise source of the savings.

D. Assigns the savings within the bidder's organization in the appropriate segments in the business system.

4. Which of the following are true concerning the capturing of synergies from an acquisition?

   I. Improvements generally come over the long run and do not appear until after the first year.

   II. Explicit costs to consider are the cost of decommissioning plants and severance pay.

   III. Acquirers often underestimate benefits and do not capture all available synergies.

   IV. Implicit costs include rebranding campaigns and the cost of integrating technologies.

   A. I and II only.

   B. I and IV only.

   C. I, II, and III only.

   D. II and IV only.

5. When an acquiring firm is making the decision whether to offer cash or stock for a target, it should be more inclined to offer cash if:

   I. The stock market is in a bubble.

   II. There is a higher level of confidence in the acquisition creating value.

   III. The acquiring firm has relatively low debt-to-equity ratios.

   IV. The target is larger.

   A. I and II only.

   B. I and IV only.

   C. II and III only.

   D. III and IV only.

6. Which of the following is most accurate concerning the findings of the study of 90 acquisitions by McKinsey's Merger and Management practice (as illustrated in Exhibit 21.8 in the text).

   A. Managers were better able to realize estimated cost savings than estimated revenue increases.

   B. Managers were better able to realize estimated revenue increases than estimated cost savings.

   C. Managers were able to realize estimated cost savings and estimated revenue increases fairly well and about equally well.

   D. Managers were not able to realize estimated cost savings nor estimated revenue increases with any success.

7. With respect to the wavelike behavior of acquisitions, list the three market conditions that have led to a rise in the number of acquisitions.

   A. _____

   B. _____

   C. _____

8. In the following list, identify whether the indicated activity is one of the archetypical strategies that has a higher probability of creating value or one of the more difficult strategies for creating value. Write "Archetypical" or "Difficult" in the blanks.

   A. Accelerating market access for target's or buyer's products: _____ _____

   B. Picking winners early and helping them develop their business: _____ _____

   C. Consolidating to improve competitive behavior: _____

   D. Consolidating to remove excess capacity from industry: _____

   E. Using a roll-up strategy: _____

   F. Improving the target company's performance: _____

   G. Entering into a transformational merger: _____

   H. Buying cheap: _____

   I. Getting skills or technologies faster or at a lower cost: _____

9. A firm is considering making an acquisition with either borrowed cash or issued stock. With the cash acquisition, the earnings per share (EPS) after the acquisition will increase 20 percent. The stock acquisition will increase EPS only 10 percent. Even so, explain why the purchase with cash can destroy more value or create less value than the purchase with stock.

10. With reference to Question 9, what is the general implication concerning the importance of accounting measures in assessing the possible benefits and the appropriate strategy for an acquisition?

11. Exhibit 21.6 in the text presents a list of cost-saving categories by function for a generic firm. List the six functions and give at least two examples for each function.

Function	Examples
1.	i.
	ii.
2.	i.
	ii.
3.	i.
	ii.
4.	i.
	ii.
5.	i.
	ii.
6.	i.
	ii.

12. An all-equity firm worth $100 billion acquires for $8 billion cash a firm whose postacquisition value will be $10 billion. The acquiring firm had the cash and did not need to borrow. The current market value of the target is $6 billion. What is the estimated return to the shareholders of the acquiring firm and to the shareholders of the target firm?

22

Creating Value
through Divestitures

Managers should devote as much time to divestitures as they do to acquisitions; however, managers tend to delay divesting, which leads to the loss of potential value creation. Divestments can create value both around the time of the announcement and in the long term. A divestiture creates value because of the "best owner" principle whereby the old owner's culture or expertise is not well suited for the needs of the divested business. A mature parent company divesting an innovative growth division is the typical example; however, companies ripe for divestiture could be at any stage in their life cycle.

Considerations in divesting are (1) possible losses from synergies and shared assets and systems; (2) financing and fiscal changes; (3) legal, contractual, and regulatory barriers; and (4) the pricing and liquidity of assets. The costs from synergy losses, for example, may be subtle, and existing contracts may have to be renegotiated. Evidence shows that the level of liquidity of the divested assets plays a role in the amount of value created.

Divestitures can be private transactions, such as trade sales and joint ventures, or they can be public transactions. Private transactions generally lead to more value creation for the seller. Public transactions include IPOs, carve-outs, spin-offs (demergers), split-offs, and the issuance of a tracking stock. Public transactions can be beneficial over the long term if the industry is consolidating. Several types of public transactions often generate negative returns, however, and the divestiture is usually temporary. In the case of carve-outs, for example, the market-adjusted long-term performance for carve-out parents and subsidiaries is usually negative, and usually minority carve-outs are eventually fully sold or reacquired.

For Questions 1 through 10, answer True or False.

1. Both divestitures and acquisitions occur in waves.

2. Managers devote as much time to divestitures as they do to acquisitions.

3. Companies that employ a balanced portfolio approach to acquisitions and divestures have outperformed companies that rarely divest.

4. The liquidity of the assets of the divested company plays a role in the amount of value created.

5. Combining various businesses with different operating risk profiles may result in a group with a higher relative debt capacity than some of the businesses individually are able to sustain.

6. After most divestments, at least initially, the parent company maintains control over the business unit.

7. The possibility of dilution appears to play a role in managers' willingness to divest.

8. A profitable, cash-generating business and a high-growth business can be candidates for divestiture.

9. Tracking stocks are more popular than carve-outs and spin-offs because they do a better job of delivering the benefits sought by managers.

10. Fiscal changes may be difficult to assess, and they can have real impact on the postdeal economics of a divestiture.

11. Which of the following is *not* true concerning spin-offs?
    A. Overall, they have not created value for the parent companies.
    B. Overall, they have created value for the spin-offs.
    C. The parent company gives up control of the subsidiary.
    D. Whether or not the spin-off is a focus-improving strategy is important with respect to value creation.

12. According to Exhibit 22.5 in the text, which of the following trajectories had a positive median market-adjusted return?
    I. Those that eventually became independent.
    II. Those that eventually merged with or were acquired by other companies.

    III. Those that were reacquired by the parent.

    IV. Those that were delisted.

       A. I only.

       B. I and III only.

       C. II and III only.

       D. I, II, III, and IV.

13. When a parent company is planning to divest and is making a choice between a public and a private transaction, if the goal is to capture value more quickly, which is usually the better choice?

    A. A public transaction.

    B. A private transaction.

    C. Neither has a good record of capturing value quickly.

    D. Neither, because each captures value about as quickly as the other.

14. Which of the following is most accurate concerning the losses and impediments caused by legal, contractual, or regulatory barriers in the divestment process?

    A. They can greatly distort the value creation and seriously slow down the process.

    B. They do not greatly distort the value creation, but they do seriously slow down the process.

    C. They can greatly distort the value creation, but generally do not slow down the process.

    D. They neither distort the value creation nor seriously slow down the process.

15. Which of the following is *not* true concerning tracking stocks?

    A. They create a separate class of parent shares.

    B. They are distributed to existing parent shareholders.

    C. It is a way to keep the liabilities of the parent and subsidiary separate.

    D. The parent company maintains control of the subsidiary.

16. For each type of divestiture, indicate if it is a public or private divestiture and select the letter associated with the closest definition from the list following the table. One definition does not belong on the list.

Type of divestiture	Public or private?	Definition (letter from list)
Trade sale		
Spin-off		
Split-off		
Carve-out		
IPO		
Joint venture		

A. A combination of part or all of a business with other industry players, other companies in the value chain, or venture capitalists.

B. Sale of part of the shares in a subsidiary to new shareholders in the stock market.

C. Distribution of all shares in a subsidiary to existing shareholders of the parent company.

D. Sale of part or all of a business to a strategic or financial investor.

E. Government outright purchase of subsidiary by eminent domain.

F. Sale of all shares of a subsidiary to new shareholders in the stock market.

G. An offer to existing shareholders of the parent company to exchange their shares for shares in the subsidiary.

23

Capital Structure

Managers should manage capital structure with the goal of not destroying value as opposed to trying to create value. There is usually more to lose than to gain when making a decision in this area. There are three levels of decisions: (1) determining strategic funding needs, (2) determining a target, and (3) choosing short-term tactical steps to adjust the capital structure when needed. Managers have many choices concerning capital structure (e.g., using equity, straight debt, convertibles, and off-balance-sheet financing). Managers can create value from using tools other than equity and straight debt under only a few conditions. Even when using more exotic forms of financing like convertibles and preferred stock, fundamentally it is a choice between debt and equity.

Managers must recognize the many trade-offs to both the firm and investors when choosing between debt and equity financing. The firm increases risk but saves on taxes by using debt; however, investing in debt rather than equity probably increases the tax liability to investors. Debt has been shown to impose a discipline on managers and discourage overinvestment, but it can also lead to business erosion and bankruptcy. Higher debt increases the conflicts among the stakeholders. Most companies choose a capital structure that gives them a credit rating between BBB– and A+, which indicates these are effective ratings, and capital structure does not have a large effect on value in most cases. It is true, however, that capital structure can make a difference for companies at the far end of the coverage spectrum.

Credit ratings have three uses: (1) they are a useful summary indicator of capital structure health, (2) they determine a company's access to credit markets, and (3) they are a means of communicating information to shareholders. The two main determinants of credit ratings are size and interest coverage. Two important coverage ratios are the EBITA-to-interest ratio and the debt-to-EBITDA ratio. The former is a short-term measure, and the latter is more useful for long-term planning. The ratio of debt to debt plus equity—that is, $D/(D + E)$—is basically a long-term measure of EBITA to interest.

Managers must weigh the benefits of managing capital structure against the costs of the choices and the possible signals the choices send to investors. Methods to manage capital structure include changing the dividends, issuing and buying back equity, and issuing and paying off debt. When designing a long-term capital structure, the firm should project surpluses and deficits, develop a target capital structure, and decide on tactical measures. The tactical, short-term tools include changing the dividend, repurchasing shares, and paying an extraordinary dividend.

1. Indicate whether the following situations are more likely to result from a higher or a lower level of leverage. Fill in the blank with "Higher" if the outcome is the result of higher leverage and "Lower" if it is the result of lower leverage.

    A. Business erosion: _____

    B. Increased investor conflicts: _____

    C. Corporate overinvestment: _____

    D. Bankruptcy: _____

    E. Tax savings for the firm: _____

    F. Tax savings for the investors: _____

    G. Focusing on growth instead of value: _____

    H. Shareholders preferring higher-risk projects: _____

2. List the order of financing choices according to the pecking-order theory.

    A. First choice: _____

    B. Second choice: _____

    C. Third choice: _____

    Explain the evidence for or against the pecking-order theory.

3. Using the information in Exhibit 23.2 in the text, rank the following from highest to lowest in terms of the proportion of firms with these specific ratings: BB, A, BBB, AAA.

    _____ (highest)

    _____

    _____

    _____ (lowest)

4. Rank the following, from highest to lowest, with respect to their importance in determining credit ratings.

   A. Size.

   B. Use of a complex capital structure.

   C. Coverage.

5. What is the market-based ratings approach? Why might it be superior to using ratings to assess a firm's creditworthiness?

6. Indicate whether each of the following generally has a positive or a negative effect on share price. Put a "+" or "−" in each blank.

   A. Dividend increase: _____

   B. Issuing debt: _____

   C. Issuing equity: _____

   D. Extraordinary dividend: _____

   E. Share repurchase: _____

   F. Dividend decrease: _____

   G. Debt repayment: _____

   H. Initiating dividend payments: _____

7. List the three conditions that justify a nonfinancial firm's use of derivatives to hedge risk.

   A. _____

   B. _____

   C. _____

8. Explain the conditions under which it would make sense for a firm to issue convertible debt. Explain why high-growth companies tend to use convertible debt more than other companies.

   A. Convertible debt makes sense when:

   _____

   _____

   _____

B. High-growth companies tend to use more convertible debt because:

_____

_____

_____

9. Based on the information in Exhibit 23.1 in the text, list two reasons why enterprise value initially increases as leverage increases from zero:

A. _____

B. _____

List two reasons that enterprise value decreases as leverage increases beyond a certain point:

A. _____

B. _____

10. Explain why well-managed and profitable companies appear to undervalue the benefits associated with an optimal capital structure.

24

Investor Communications

Managers should communicate with investors to help align the value of the stock with the intrinsic value of the company. If the stock is underpriced, a few of the negative consequences are that employees may be demoralized, the stock is less useful in stock acquisitions, and the firm may become a takeover target. If the stock is overpriced, the price will eventually fall, which will lead to a fall in employee morale and increased tension between the board of directors and the managers. Also, once the stock is overpriced, managers may engage in value-destroying activities in an attempt to prop up the stock price. Three ways many companies can improve investor communications are: (1) monitor the gap between price and intrinsic value, (2) understand the investor base, and (3) tailor communications to the investors who matter most.

In general, managers should try to communicate with sophisticated intrinsic investors because the activities of these investors have the most impact on the price of the stock. Managers should provide these investors with detailed financial reports as well as specific information on the individual businesses in the company. Managers should be honest and not use gimmicks such as changing the metrics reported each period to give the most favorable numbers. Furthermore, earnings guidance does not provide any discernible benefits.

1. Which of the following is most accurate concerning a common error managers make in communicating to investors?

    A. In managers' attempts to communicate with investors, they often choose to use finance experts who have poor public relations skills.

    B. Managers do not put much effort into communicating with investors.

C. In managers' attempts to communicate with investors, they often choose to use public relations experts who do not understand finance.

D. Managers generally supply too much information in a disorganized manner, which confuses investors.

2. In reporting financial information, companies should provide detailed income statement analysis for:

A. Each unit down to at least EBITA.

B. The whole aggregate firm to at least EBITA.

C. Each unit's sales and cash costs.

D. The whole aggregate firm's sales and cash costs.

3. With respect to transparency, which of the following statements are true?

I. Managers tend to avoid transparency for fear of revealing information that competitors can use.

II. Investors tend to reward firms that offer more transparency.

III. Managers respond to the increases in transparency of other firms.

IV. Managers respond to demands for increased transparency from investors.

A. I, II, and III only.

B. I, II, and IV only.

C. II, III, and IV only.

D. I, II, III, and IV.

4. Of the thousands of companies analyzed by the authors over the years, in approximately what percentage of the cases has the market value been reasonably close to an objective, thorough assessment of the company's intrinsic value, or any gap been attributable to the market's misvaluation of an entire industry?

A. 50 percent.

B. 65 percent.

C. 80 percent.

D. 95 percent.

5. With respect to growth versus value stocks, which of the following are true?

I. Most managers would like their firms to be growth stocks.

II. Growth stocks are those that have higher book and earnings multiples.

III. Most stocks labeled as growth stocks grow earnings and revenues faster than value stocks do.

IV. Most stocks labeled as growth stocks have higher ROICs.

    A. I and II only.

    B. II and III only.

    C. I, II, and IV only.

    D. I, III, and IV only.

6. Indicate in each of the following cases whether the statement concerning earnings guidance is True or False.

    A. There isn't an expected change in total return to shareholders in the first year that managers begin to offer earnings guidance.

    B. Managers engage in earnings guidance to lower share price volatility.

    C. It has been proven that earnings guidance can increase liquidity.

    D. Firms that engage in earnings guidance have higher multiples such as enterprise-value/EBITA ratio.

    E. Managers will gain advantages from providing guidance at the start of the financial year on the real short-, medium-, and long-term value drivers of their businesses.

7. Indicate in each of the following cases whether the statement concerning the type of information a firm should reveal is True or False.

    A. A mining company should emphasize production targets more than expected commodity prices.

    B. Multinational companies should discuss their targets using constant currency rates.

    C. Managers of conglomerates should reveal aggregate numbers rather than business-by-business numbers.

    D. Managers should provide ranges rather than point estimates.

    E. Managers across industries should strive to provide information on a common set of value drivers.

8. Identify and describe two primary benefits that a systematic approach to investor communications provides a manager.

    A. _____

        _____

    B. _____

        _____

9. Identify and describe the three key elements of a well-defined investment story.

   A. _____

   _____

   B. _____

   _____

   C. _____

   _____

10. Define the term *transparency* as it relates to corporate investor communications.

25

Taxes

In estimating value, an analyst needs to determine the portion of taxes due from the operating activities, then determine the operating cash taxes, and, finally, estimate the value of the corporation recognizing that some taxes are deferred. The available information on the analyzed firm will be incomplete; therefore, analysts can only estimate the operating cash taxes, and the estimates will have errors. Using either the company's statutory tax rate or the company's effective rate with no adjustments is not appropriate for computing operating taxes. One suitable approach is to compute taxes as if the company were financed entirely with equity. To accomplish this task, an analyst could begin with reported taxes and undo financing and nonoperating items one by one. The analyst should make estimates based on the tax rates in the various jurisdictions in which the firm operates.

Estimates of operating taxes actually paid in cash provide a better input for valuation than those estimates that include accruals. As part of the estimation process, the analyst should subtract the increase in net operating deferred tax liabilities (DTLs) from operating taxes. Information for this process should be in the tax footnote. Also, the reorganized balance sheet needs to properly assign deferred tax assets (DTAs) and deferred tax liabilities. For each deferred tax account, there are four valuation methodologies: (1) value the account as part of NOPLAT, (2) value the account as part of a corresponding nonoperating asset or liability, (3) value the account as a separate nonoperating asset, and (4) ignore the account as an accounting convention.

For Questions 1 through 8, answer True or False.

1. With full information, operating taxes can be computed without error.

2. The effects of research and development should be removed from operating taxes.

3. Operating taxes are computed as if the company were financed entirely with equity.

4. It is not correct to use the company's effective tax rate with no adjustments.

5. The income tax footnote is a good source of information for deferred tax liabilities.

6. All deferred tax liabilities are classified as debt.

7. Usually, a company will record a DTL during the year of an acquisition and then draw down the DTL as the intangible amortizes.

8. Making estimates of operating taxes based on tax rates in individual jurisdictions is not recommended.

9. Of the list of deferred tax assets and liabilities (i.e., DTAs and DTLs), indicate whether each is a DTA or a DTL and whether it should be classified as operating or nonoperating.

Account	DTA or DTL?	Operating or nonoperating?
Nondeductible intangibles		
Tax loss carry-forwards		
Accelerated depreciation		
Pension and postretirement benefits		
Warranty reserves		

10. Complete the table by filling in the blank cells. The ultimate goal is to compute the effective tax rate and the operating tax rate.

	Domestic subsidiary	Foreign subsidiary	R&D tax credits	One-time credits	Company
EBITA	3,000	800			
Amortization	(1,000)	(200)			
EBIT					
Interest expense	(800)	(200)			
Gains on asset sales	100	0			
Earnings before taxes					
Taxes			110	88	
Net Income					
Tax rates (percent)					
Statutory rate	30%	40%			
Effective tax rate					
EBITA	3,000	800			
Operating taxes			110		
NOPLAT					
Tax rates (percent)					
Statutory rate	30%	40%			
Operating tax rate					

26

Nonoperating Expenses, One-Time Charges, Reserves, and Provisions

Strict accounting rules exist for dealing with nonoperating expenses and one-time charges. For determining value, however, these entries and the financial statements require adjustments. Despite popular belief, these entries provide relevant information concerning past performance and future cash flows. A three-step process can aid in assessing the impact of nonoperating charges: (1) reorganize the income statement into operating and nonoperating items, (2) search the notes for embedded one-time items, and (3) analyze each extraordinary item for its impact on future operations.

Noncash expenses usually lower an asset or increase a provision account in the liabilities. In evaluating a business, there are four types of provisions: (1) ongoing operating provisions, (2) long-term operating provisions, (3) nonoperating restructuring provisions, and (4) provisions created to smooth income.

1. Given the following list, indicate if each entry is an item related to the ongoing core business of a company. Enter "Yes" if it relates to the ongoing core business and "No" if it does not.

   A. Litigation-related charges: _____

   B. Royalty expense: _____

   C. Impairment of goodwill: _____

D. Restructuring charges: _____

E. SG&A expense: _____

F. R&D expense: _____

G. Loss or gain on assets: _____

H. Amortization expense: _____

I. Purchased R&D expense: _____

2. Given the following entries concerning revenues and adjustments for provisions for an asset, compute NOPLAT, invested capital, and ROIC on beginning-of-year invested capital. Assume that all invested capital entries are beginning-of-year entries and all revenue entries are for year-end.

Reserve for income smoothing = $2,500

Reported EBITA = $4,000

Increase in income-smoothing reserve = $600

Reserve for product returns = $800

Reserve for plant decommissioning = $5,000

Interest associated with plant decommissioning = $500

Provision for restructuring = $400

Reserve for restructuring = $1,000

3. A firm just built a plant that it plans to decommission in three years. It estimates the decommissioning costs in three years will be $100 million. The relevant interest rate is 8 percent. Complete the table.

Balance sheet	Year 1	Year 2	Year 3
Starting reserve	0		
Plant-decommissioning expense	30.80		
Interest cost	0		
Decommissioning payout	0	0	(100)
Ending reserve	30.80		0
Income statement			
Reported provision	30.80		

4. Explain the two classifications for acquisition premiums and how in-process R&D fits into the categories.

5. Give an example of when a litigation charge should be considered an operating charge.

6. In computing operating performance, what should the policy be toward goodwill impairments? Why?

7. Explain when the size of a nonoperating expense or one-time charge mentioned in a management discussion and analysis (MD&A) note might determine whether it should be included in the adjustment to NOPLAT. Include the reasoning for the decision.

8. In the following table there is a list of examples of provisions and reserves in column 1 (the far left column). Fill in the blank cells with the appropriate letters.

   In column 2, with respect to classification treatment, indicate which of the examples in column 1 is: (A) a nonoperating provision, (B) an income-smoothing provision, (C) an ongoing operating provision, or (D) a long-term operating provision.

   In column 3, with respect to treatment in NOPLAT, indicate which of the following corresponds to the examples in column 1: (E) deduct operating portion from revenue to determine NOPLAT and treat interest portion as nonoperating, (F) convert accrual provision into cash provision and treat as nonoperating, (G) eliminate provision by converting accrual provision into cash provision, or (H) deduct provisions from revenue to determine NOPLAT.

   In column 4, with respect to treatment in invested capital, indicate which of the following corresponds to the examples in column 1: (I) deduct reserve from operating assets to determine invested capital, (J) treat reserve as a debt equivalent, (K) (same as J) treat reserve as a debt equivalent, or (L) treat reserve as an equity equivalent.

   In column 5, with respect to treatment in valuation, indicate which of the following corresponds to the examples in column 1: (M) provision is part of free cash flow, (N) deduct reserve's present value from the value of operations, (O) not relevant, or (P) deduct reserve's present value from the value of operations.

Examples of provisions and reserves	Classification treatment	Treatment in NOPLAT	Treatment in invested capital	Treatment in valuation
Plant decommissioning costs and unfunded retirement plans				
Provisions for the sole purpose of income smoothing				
Product returns and warranties				
Restructuring charges (e.g., expected severance payouts from layoffs)				

27

Leases, Pensions, and
Other Obligations

Leases, pension obligations, and securitized receivables are like debt obligations, but accounting rules can allow them to be off-balance-sheet items. Such items can bias ROIC upward, which makes competitive benchmarking unreliable; however, valuation may be unaffected.

To adjust for operating leases, the analyst should (1) recognize the lease as both an obligation and asset on the balance sheet (which requires an increase in operating income by adding an implicit interest expense to the income statement and lowering operating expenses by the same amount), (2) adjust WACC for the new leverage ratios, and (3) value the company based on the new free cash flow and WACC. Assuming straight-line depreciation, an estimate of a leased asset's value for the balance sheet is:

$$\text{Asset value}_{t-1} = \frac{\text{Rental Expense}_t}{\left(k_d + \dfrac{1}{\text{Life of the Asset}}\right)}$$

Another source of distortion occurs when a company sells a portion of its receivables and thereby reduces accounts receivable on the balance sheet and increases cash flow from operations on the cash flow statement. Despite the favorable changes in accounting measures, the selling of receivables is very similar to increasing debt, because the company pays fees for the arrangement, it reduces its borrowing capacity, and the firm pays higher interest rates on unsecured debt. The information to make adjustments should appear in the footnotes to company accounts. The analyst should add back securitized receivables to the balance sheet and make a corresponding increase to short-term debt. These alterations will determine the necessary changes to return on capital, free cash flow, and leverage. Interest expense should increase by the fees paid for securitizing receivables.

Companies must report excess pension assets and unfunded pension obligations on the balance sheet at their current values, but pension accounting can still greatly distort operating profitability. An analyst should take three steps to incorporate excess pension assets and unfunded pension liabilities into enterprise value and the income statement to eliminate accounting distortions. Those three steps are: (1) identify excess pension assets and unfunded liabilities on the balance sheet, (2) add excess pension assets to and deduct unfunded pension liabilities from enterprise value, (3) remove the accounting pension expense from cost of sales and replace it with the service cost and amortization of prior service costs reported in the notes. Much of the necessary information for this process appears in the company's notes.

1. Match the type of off-balance-sheet liability with the type of company with which it is most likely to be associated.

Companies with few fixed assets	_____	A. Operating leases
Established companies (age > 20 years)	_____	B. Securitized receivables
Industries that use large, easily transferrable assets	_____	C. Unfunded pensions

2. Use the words "lower" or "increase" to fill in the blanks.

A profitable company has chosen to lease its assets. This move will artificially _____ operating profits. It will artificially _____ capital productivity. With respect to return on assets, it is most likely that it will _____ ROIC.

3. Indicate how an analyst's appropriate adjustments for operating leases should adjust assets, liabilities, and operating income. Fill in each blank with either "lower" or "increase."

The analyst's adjustments should _____ assets, _____ liabilities, and _____ operating income.

4. Explain the usual relationship of the interest rate used in operating lease adjustments relative to the firm's cost of debt (higher or lower) and why that relationship usually exists.

5. In making adjustments for leases, where or how would an analyst get rental expenses and the value of the leased assets?

6. Using the formula that incorporates the rental expense, asset life, and appropriate interest rate, compute the estimated value of a leased asset at the beginning of an accounting period. The rental expense for the period is $4,000, the cost of debt is 6 percent, and the asset's life is five years.

7. Identify three methods for estimating the value of leased assets other than the formula used in Question 6. In each case, indicate whether the method tends to overestimate or underestimate the value of the leased assets, and explain the reason.

   A. _____

   B. _____

   C. _____

8. Summarize the results of two extensive studies cited in the text (one by Lim, Mann, and Mihov and the other from Ohio State University) concerning how credit agencies adjust for companies that use leases and the power of credit statistics adjusted for operating leases to explain the interest rates paid by firms that use leases by answering the following questions.

   A. What are the effects of using more operating leases on the firm's credit rating and the required yield on new debt?
   _____

   B. Can operating leases help explain variations in interest rates?
   _____

   C. What does the overall evidence suggest for how investors, lenders, and rating agencies interpret operating leases?
   _____

9. Fill in the blanks in the following sentences to indicate how an analyst should adjust for securitized receivables.

To determine return on capital, free cash flow, and leverage consistently, make the following adjustments on the balance sheet: _____ _____ and _____. The fees paid for securitizing receivables should be _____ _____.

10. Complete the following sentences concerning the adjustments for pensions in valuation.

    Excess pension assets should be treated as _____, and unfunded pension liabilities should be treated as _____. With respect to taxes, valuations should be done _____.

11. Compute the operating profits and operating profits adjusted for pension liabilities and assets, given the following information. The amortized prior-year service cost and the amortization of loss are zero.

    Operating revenues = $1,000

    Operating costs = $600

    Pension interest cost = $700

    Expected return on pension plan assets = $500

    Pension service cost = $150

12. Given the following information, calculate (A) invested capital before the adjustment for leases, (B) the WACC before the adjustment for leases, (C) invested capital after the adjustment for leases, and (D) the WACC after the adjustment for leases.

    Operating assets = $3,000

    Operating liabilities = $1,000

    Book value of debt = $1,500

    Market value of debt = $1,800

    Book value of equity = $500

    Market value of equity = $900

    Operating leases = $2,000

    After-tax required return on unsecured debt = 6%

    Required return on equity (CAPM) = 13%

    After-tax required return on secured debt = 5%

    A. _____

    B. _____

    C. _____

    D. _____

28

Capitalized Expenses

Investments in intangible assets are expensed, which can introduce a negative bias in ROIC and lead managers to make incorrect decisions concerning how to create value. Investments in R&D and other intangibles should be capitalized for three reasons: (1) to represent historical investment more accurately, (2) to prevent manipulation of short-term earnings, and (3) to improve performance assessments of long-term investments. These change only the perceptions of performance, however, and will not change the value of the firm. Since free cash flow (FCF) includes both operating expenses and investment expenditures, capitalizing an expense will not affect FCF.

The process for capitalizing R&D has three steps: (1) build and amortize the R&D asset using an appropriate asset life, (2) make the appropriate upward adjustment on invested capital, and (3) make the appropriate upward adjustment on NOPLAT. An analyst can apply these adjustments to other expenses, such as an expansion of distribution routes. A couple of drawbacks of making too many such adjustments are the increased ability to manipulate short-term performance and the incentives for managers not to recognize when to write down an asset created from a capitalized expense.

1. Explain how ROIC with R&D capitalized will compare to R&D expensed over the life of a firm. Which will be higher at different points in the firm's life? Will either or both eventually stabilize? (Hint: See Exhibit 28.2 in the text.)

2. Based on your answer to Question 1, explain why it is so important for an analyst to adjust ROIC when making decisions. (Hint: What are the two drivers of value?)

3. Based on Exhibit 28.3 in the text, how do the ROICs compare when using an estimated asset life of 12 years instead of six years? What are the implications of this comparison for choosing an estimated life of an R&D expense in the capitalization process?

4. Based on Exhibit 28.3, compare the general relationship of ROIC to changing asset life for when R&D is 5 percent of revenues and when R&D is 15 percent of revenues. Is the relationship very different? Compute the proportional declines from extending the life from two to four years and from extending it from 10 to 12 years. What are the implications of a comparison of the results?

5. Complete the following table for years 3 and 4 to demonstrate how ROIC adjusted for capitalized R&D will eventually fall below unadjusted ROIC. The assumptions are that growth of revenues is 10 percent each year, production expenses are 50 percent of revenue, R&D is 5 percent of revenue, and investment in physical assets is 20 percent. Investments are depreciated 10 percent each year. There are no taxes. The difference between unadjusted and adjusted initial capital, 2,000 and 2,180 respectively, reflects capitalized R&D from previous years.

Year	1	2	3	4
Sales	1,000	1,100		
Production expenses	(500)	(550)		
R&D	(50)	(55)		
Depreciation	(200)	(200)		
Operating income	250	295		
Initial capital	2,000	2,000		
Investment	(200)	(220)		
ROIC	12.50%			
Adj. initial capital	2,180	2,212		
Adj. depreciation	(218)	(221.2)		
Adj. operating income	282	328.8		
Adj. ROIC	12.94%			

29

Inflation

Inflation makes analyzing performance and making comparisons difficult. Also, inflation usually impedes the creation of value. Inflation lowers the value of monetary assets, and the firm can rarely pass along the full effects of inflation to customers. Typically ROIC does not increase enough to compensate the firm for inflation. The increase in inflation from the 1960s to the 1970s was accompanied by a decline in P/E ratios.

During periods of high inflation, the problem becomes much worse. An analyst needs to correct for the following distortions: (1) overstated growth, (2) overestimated capital turnover, (3) overstated operating margins, and (4) distorted credit ratios. When making forecasts in such periods, the analyst can make adjustments in either nominal or real terms, but consistent financial projections require elements of both nominal and real forecasts. Five steps for making forecasts in periods of high inflation are: (1) forecast operating performance in real terms, (2) build financial statements in nominal terms, (3) build financial statements in real terms, (4) forecast free cash flow (FCF) in real and nominal terms, and (5) estimate discounted cash flow (DCF) value in real and nominal terms.

1. Given the following list, indicate for which items real or nominal modeling applications are preferred. Put "Real" or "Nominal" in each blank.

   A. EBITA   _____

   B. Sales   _____

   C. Income taxes   _____

    D. EBITDA   _____

    E. Financial statements   _____

    F. Investments in working capital   _____

    G. Capital expenditures   _____

2. Identify three effects of volatile inflation on estimating cash flows.

    A. _____

    B. _____

    C. _____

3. Identify and describe three adjustments to the enterprise DCF and economic profit when attempting to establish the value of a company located in an environment of high inflation.

    A. _____

    B. _____

    C. _____

4. Discuss the need for both real and nominal forecasts:

    A. Real forecasts:_____

    _____

    B. Nominal forecasts:_____

    _____

5. Identify the five-step approach managers should employ to combine nominal and real forecasts.

    A. _____

    B. _____

    C. _____

    D. _____

    E. _____

6. Given the following information, compute FCF in real terms:

Real growth is 4 percent, real ROIC is 10 percent, real NOPLAT is $2,000, real networking capital from the previous year is $1,000, the inflation index last year was 200, and the inflation index this year is 300.

7. A firm begins with nominal $NWC^N_{t-1} = 100$ and then doubles it to $NWC^N_t = 200$. The price index increases from $IX_{t-1} = 2$ to $IX_t = 2.5$. Based on this information, what is the real investment in NWC in year t?

8. Given the following information, compute the real continuing value:

   Real ROIC is 6 percent, real NOPLAT is $3,000, nominal WACC is 21 percent, inflation is 10 percent, real growth is 4 percent, real net working capital is $1,500, and real invested capital is $10,000.

9. Follow the procedures in Exhibit 29.3 in the text to fill in the blanks in the following table and demonstrate that FCF will fall even when the firm increases EBITA at the rate of inflation. Inflation is 20 percent. The firm has a policy of replacing assets at the rate of depreciation, which is 10 percent per year.

	Year 1	Year 2
Sales	2,000	2,100
EBITDA	600	
Depreciation	400	
EBITA	200	
Gross property, plant, and equipment	4,000	
Cumulative depreciation	2,500	2,500
Invested capital	1,500	
EBITDA	600	
Capital expenditures	400	
Free cash flow (FCF)	200	
EBITA growth (percent)	–	
EBITA/sales (percent)		
Return on invested capital (percent)		
FCF growth (percent)	–	

10. The effect of differential growth on revenues can be examined by splitting revenue growth into real and inflation components. Forecast revenue so that revenue (year 2) = revenue (year 1) × (1 + real growth rate) × (1 + inflation rate). Following are the assumptions for the analysis.

Assumptions	Year 1	Year 2	Year 3	Year 4	Year 5 onward
Real revenue growth		5%	5%	5%	1%
EBITDA/revenue	0.3	0.3	0.3	0.3	0.3
Tax rate	0.5	0.5	0.5	0.5	0.5
Depreciation/net PPE (beginning of year)	0.2	0.2	0.2	0.2	0.2
Net PPE (end of year/revenues)	0.4	0.4	0.4	0.4	0.4
Working capital/revenues	0.2	0.2	0.2	0.2	0.2
Inflation rate	20%	50%	20%	10%	5%
Inflation index	1	1.5	1.8	1.98	

A. Project NOPLAT, invested capital, and free cash flow on an unadjusted deflated basis for 15 years, by deflating revenues only.

Pro forma financials	Unadjusted deflated forecasts				Cont. value
	1	2	3	4	15
Revenues	1,000				
EBITDA					
Depreciation					
Operating income					
Tax					
NOPLAT					
Working capital					
Net PPE (beginning of year)	350				
Less: Depreciation	(70)				
Plus: Capex					
Net PPE (end of year)					
Invested capital					
EBITDA					
Less: Tax					
Less: Capex					
Less: Working capital increase					
Free cash flow					

B. Project NOPLAT, invested capital, and free cash flow on a nominal basis for 15 years.

Pro forma financials	Nominal forecasts				Cont. value
	1	2	3	4	15
Revenues	1,000				
EBITDA					
Depreciation					
Operating income					
Tax					
NOPLAT					
Working capital					
Net PPE (beginning of year)	350				
Less: Depreciation	(70)				
Plus: Capex					
Net PPE (end of year)					
Invested capital					
EBITDA					
Less: Tax					
Less: Capex					
Less: Working capital increase					
Free cash flow					

C. Project NOPLAT, invested capital, and free cash flow for 15 years.

Pro forma financials	Real forecasts				Cont. value
	1	2	3	4	15
Revenues	1,000				
EBITDA					
Depreciation					
Operating income					
Tax					
NOPLAT					
Working capital					
Net PPE (beginning of year)	350				
Less: Depreciation	(70)				
Plus: Capex					
Net PPE (end of year)					
Invested capital					

(Continued)

(Continued)

	Real forecasts				Cont. value
Pro forma financials	**1**	**2**	**3**	**4**	**15**
EBITDA					
Less: Tax					
Less: Capex					
Less: Working capital increase					
Free cash flow					

D. Compare the approaches using the following results template.

	Forecasts				Cont. value
Unadjusted deflated	**1**	**2**	**3**	**4**	**15**
Real NOPLAT					
Real free cash flow					
Invested capital/revenue					
ROIC pretax					
ROIC posttax					
Nominal					
Real NOPLAT					
Real free cash flow					
Invested capital/revenue					
ROIC pretax					
ROIC posttax					
Real					
Real NOPLAT					
Real free cash flow					
Invested capital/revenue					
ROIC pretax					
ROIC posttax					

11. Given the free cash flow developed in the previous question, compute the indicated measures. Use an 8 percent real cost of capital.

   A. Compute the continuing value nominal weighted cost of capital.

   B. Compute the continuing value nominal growth rate.

C. Calculate unadjusted deflated forecast DCF.

		Forecasts				Cont. value
Results	**1**	**2**	**3**	**4**	**5–14**	**15**
Real WACC						
Unadjusted deflated free cash flow						
Continuing value						
Discount factor						
PV of free cash flow						
Unadjusted deflated DCF						

Free cash flow for years 1 to 15 is to be taken directly from the free cash flow forecast from Question 6. Continuing value is discounted by the real WACC net of the real growth rate in perpetuity.

D. Calculate nominal forecast DCF.

		Forecasts				Cont. value
Results	**1**	**2**	**3**	**4**	**5–14**	**15**
Nominal WACC						
Nominal free cash flow						
Continuing value						
Discount factor						
PV of free cash flow						
Nominal DCF						

E. Calculate real forecast DCF.

		Forecasts				Cont. value
Results	**1**	**2**	**3**	**4**	**5–14**	**15**
Real WACC						
Real free cash flow						
Continuing value						
Discount factor						
PV of free cash flow						
Real DCF						

Foreign Currency

U.S. Generally Accepted Accounting Principles (GAAP) and International Financial Reporting Standards (IFRS) have been converging over time, and the valuation of companies and subsidiaries in foreign countries has become easier. Yet an analyst needs to consider four issues when analyzing foreign companies: (1) making forecasts in foreign and domestic currencies, (2) estimating the cost of capital in a foreign currency, (3) incorporating foreign-currency risk in valuations, and (4) using translated foreign-currency financial statements.

For a given company, the analyst should forecast the cash flows in the most relevant currency. Then, the analyst should use either the spot-rate method or the forward-rate method to convert the value of the cash flows into that of the parent company. It is important to use consistent monetary assumptions in the process (e.g., concerning inflation and interest rates). When estimating the cost of capital, the analyst should use the equity premium from a global portfolio without an adjustment for currency risk. When translating statements into another currency, there are three choices: the current method, the temporal method, and the inflation-adjusted current method. Usually, the current method is the most appropriate approach.

1. Identify the currency translation method to use in treating a foreign subsidiary in each of the following cases.

   A. The analyst is using U.S. GAAP and the country of the subsidiary is experiencing hyperinflation.

   B. The analyst is using IFRS and the country of the subsidiary is experiencing moderate inflation.

C. The analyst is using U.S. GAAP and the country of the subsidiary is experiencing moderate inflation.

D. The analyst is using IFRS and the country of the subsidiary is experiencing hyperinflation.

2. Describe the foreign-currency method for evaluating a foreign subsidiary and explain why the forward-rate method is more complex than the spot-rate method in estimating the value. Include in the discussion the steps needed to remedy possible problems.

3. List and summarize the three categories of assumptions needed when making projections of and discounting cash flows in different currencies.

A. _____

B. _____

C. _____

4. Summarize the main point of Exhibit 30.4 in the text.

5. Complete the table using the procedures in Exhibit 30.1 in the text. One value has been provided in most rows to help you get started in the process.

Monetary Data for Computing the Present Value of a Norwegian Subsidiary of an American Corporation

	2010	2011	2012	2013	2014	2015
Foreign currency (Norwegian kroner—NOK)						
Cash flows						
Nominal cash flow	300	320	340	365	395	440
Real cash flow	297					
Inflation (percent)	1.00	2.00	2.00	3.00	3.00	3.00
Interest rates (percent)						
Real interest rate	2.00	2.00	2.00	2.00	2.00	2.00
Nominal forward interest rate				5.06		
Nominal interest yield						4.38

(Continued)

(Continued)

	2010	2011	2012	2013	2014	2015
Spot exchange rate NOK/USD	5					
Forward exchange rate					4.62	
Domestic currency (U.S. dollars—USD)						
Interest rates						
Nominal interest yield				5.57		
Nominal forward interest rate		5.06				
Real interest rate	3.00	3.00	3.00	3.00	3.00	3.00
Inflation (percent)	2.00	2.00	3.00	3.00	4.00	4.00
Cash flows						
Real cash flow					82.13	
Nominal cash flow		65.91				

6. Using the information from Question 5, fill in the table and compute the present value of the cash flows in dollars using the spot-rate method and the forward-rate method.

Discounted Cash Flows and Present Value of Subsidiary

NOK discount rate

PV of NOK cash flows

Sum of PV of NOK cash flows

PV of NOK CFs × Spot rate

USD discount rate

PV of NOK CFs × Forward rates

Sum of PV of USD cash flows

31

Case Study: Heineken

Analyzing a company's future performance and estimating its value begins with examining historical and current data and then making projections. An analyst should make several sets of forecasts or scenarios using different assumptions concerning the business environment and the strategy of the firm. A simple example is where an analyst creates only two or three scenarios (e.g., a business-as-usual scenario, an aggressive marketing or acquisition scenario, and an operational improvement scenario). Each scenario would have its own focus, such as customer segmentation analysis, industry structure analysis, or business system analysis.

The analyst should estimate value using various explicit forecast horizons and different methods. Recall from earlier chapters that there are usually two periods to forecast: the explicit forecast period and the period after that in which the challenge is to estimate the continuing value for that period. There is also the choice of using the free cash flow (FCF) method and the economic-profit method for estimating value. The analyst should use both methods and compare the results. By estimating value using different explicit forecast horizons and methods, the analyst can verify that the model is robust and the assumptions are consistent.

1. Discuss how customer segmentation analysis, business system analysis, and industry structure analysis contribute to a better understanding of the value added for the firm.

   A. Customer segmentation analysis:

   _____

   _____

   B. Business system analysis:

   _____

   _____

   C. Industry structure analysis:

   _____

   _____

2. Given the following historical data, forecast Saws and Drills Corporation's FCF for the conservative scenario in the first template (A) and the aggressive scenario in the second template (B).

Saws and Drills Corporation

	2006	2007	2008	2009	2010
Current assets	499	489	443	429	484
Current liabilities	240	236	255	237	369
Debt in current liabilities	25	12	7	21	78
Long-term debt	218	200	244	207	236
Total assets	686	693	598	579	730
Capital expenditures	34	34	16	18	23
Change in deferred taxes	4	(5)	3	2	2
Sales	851	838	754	789	1,029
Operating expenses	626	624	579	592	765
General expenses	151	157	132	134	191
Depreciation	23	24	24	21	26
Investment income	4	2	2	3	2
Interest expense	22	20	19	19	16
Miscellaneous income, net	3	(33)	(75)	–	(70)
Income taxes	18	4	10	11	8

   A. Conservative: Saws and Drills Corporation is barely able to hold its own in the global arena of faster-paced technological change and customer demands.

   Goal: Maintain historical sales, operating, and general expense structures: operating expense/sales of 74 percent in perpetuity, SG&A/sales

of 18.6 percent, taxes of 40 percent, working capital/sales of 18.15 percent, net fixed assets of 24 percent, and three years of sales growth at 20 percent per year.

| | Historic | | Forecast | |
Conservative	2010	2011	2012	2013
Working capital				
Net fixed assets				
Invested capital				
Net investment				
Debt				
Equity				
Sales growth		20.00%	20.00%	20.00%
Net sales	1,029.00			
Operating expense				
SG&A				
Depreciation				
Operating income				
Taxes on EBIT				
Change in deferred tax				
NOPLAT				
ROIC				
Debt/invested capital		65.00%	65.00%	65.00%
Equity/invested capital				
Tax rate		40.00%	40.00%	40.00%
Interest rate		6.00%	7.00%	7.00%
Growth (investment/capital)				
Investment rate (growth/ROIC)				
EBIT/sales				
Sales/invested capital				
Working capital/sales		18.750%	18.750%	18.750%
NFA/sales				
Operating expense/sales		75.000%	75.000%	75.000%
SG&A/sales		18.600%	18.600%	18.600%
Depreciation/sales		2.527%	2.527%	2.527%
Change in deferred tax/sales		0.194%	0.194%	0.194%
Free cash flow				

B. Aggressive: Saws and Drills Corporation introduces significant changes and increases to its product line and ability to meet technological change in the industry.

Goal: Improve all expense structures at high levels of sales growth over the near term; operating expense/sales of 74 percent, 73 percent,

73 percent for three years; SG&A/sales of 16 percent; depreciation/sales of 2.5 percent; taxes of 40 percent; working capital/sales of 18.75 percent; net fixed assets of 24 percent; and three years of sales growth of 40 percent per year.

Aggressive	Historic 2010	2011	2012	Forecast 2013
Working capital				
Net fixed assets				
Invested capital				
Net investment				
Debt				
Equity				
Sales growth		40.00%	40.00%	40.00%
Net sales	1,029.000			
Operating expense				
SG&A				
Depreciation				
Operating income				
Taxes on EBIT				
Change in deferred tax				
NOPLAT				
ROIC				
Debt/invested capital		65.00%	65.00%	65.00%
Equity/invested capital				
Tax rate		40.00%	40.00%	40.00%
Interest rate		6.00%	7.00%	7.00%
Growth (investment/capital)				
Investment rate (growth/ROIC)				
EBIT/sales				
Sales/invested capital				
Working capital/sales		18.750%	18.750%	18.750%
NFA/sales				
Operating expense/sales		74.000%	73.000%	73.000%
SG&A/sales		16.000%	16.000%	16.000%
Depreciation/sales		2.500%	2.500%	2.500%
Change in deferred tax/sales		0.194%	0.194%	0.194%
Free cash flow				

3. Demonstrate how choosing different explicit forecast horizons can give the same estimate of value. To do this, fill in the following tables where the first half of the template has a three-year explicit forecast horizon, and

the second half of the template has a five-year explicit forecast horizon. For the first year, the forecasts are NOPLAT = $10.00, depreciation = $2.50, and gross investment = $13.61; and they are already in the table. The forecasts for ROIC, NOPLAT growth, and WACC are also in the table.

Assumptions	Years 1–3 (%)	Years 4+ (%)
ROIC	18.00	11.00
NOPLAT growth	20.00	7.00
WACC	14.00	12.00

3-Year Horizon	1	2	3	CV Base
NOPLAT	10.00			
Depreciation	2.50	___	___	
Gross cash flow				
Gross investment	(13.61)	___	___	
Free cash flow				
Discount factor				
Present value FCF				
PV FCF 1–3				
PV CV	___			
Total value				

5-Year Horizon	1	2	3	4	5	CV Base
NOPLAT						
Depreciation	___	___	___	___	___	
Gross cash flow						
Gross investment	___	___	___	___	___	
Free cash flow						
Discount factor						
Present value FCF						
PV FCF 1–3						
PV CV	___					
Total value						

Compare your computed value for both time horizons. Provide an explanation of your results.

4. Fill in the following template to demonstrate the equivalence between free cash flow and economic profit (EP) estimates of value with a model similar to the three-year horizon model in Question 3.

Assumptions	Years 1–3 (%)	Years 4+ (%)
ROIC	18.00	15.75
Growth	20.00	5.00
WACC	14.00	12.00

3-Year Horizon	1	2	3	CV Base
NOPLAT	10.00			
Net investment	−11.11	_____	_____	
Free cash flow				
Beginning invested capital				
Net investment	_____	_____	_____	
New invested capital				
NOPLAT				
Capital charge	_____	_____	_____	
Economic profit				
Discount factor				
Present value FCF				
Present value EP				
PV FCF 1–3				
PV CV FCF	_____			
Total value				
PV FCF 1–3				
PV CV				
Invested capital				
Total value	_____			

32

Valuing Flexibility

Net present values (NPVs) calculated from single cash flow projections may be inadequate because they do not take into account the ability to expand or scale back. The following is a simple example where a firm can scale back by eliminating a negative cash flow project after the first period. There is a 60 percent probability of $20 per year forever or 40 percent probability of –$3 per year forever. The discount rate is 10 percent. If the initial cost today is $100, then without an option to cancel the NPV would be:

$$-\$100 + 0.6 \times (\$20/0.10) + 0.4 \times (-\$6/0.10) = -\$4$$

With the option to abandon after the first year, the NPV would be:

$$-\$100 + 0.6 \times (\$20/0.10) + 0.4 \times (-\$6/1.10) = \$17.82$$

The value of the option to cancel the project is the difference, or $21.82.

The inclusion of flexibility into the analysis is generally more relevant in the valuation of individual businesses and projects. The real-option valuation (ROV) and decision tree analysis (DTA) are the two primary methods of valuation. Both depend on forecasting based on contingent states of the world. Although ROV is typically better than DTA, it is not the right approach in every case.

1. The value of flexibility is greatest when:
    A. Uncertainty is high and managers can react to new information.
    B. Uncertainty is low and managers can react to new information.

    C. Uncertainty is high and managers cannot react to new information.

    D. Uncertainty is low and managers cannot react to new information.

2. The option to defer an investment is most like:

    A. A futures contract on a bond.

    B. A swap contract.

    C. A put option on a stock.

    D. A call option on a stock.

3. A project has a 50/50 chance of generating either a positive cash flow of $1 per year forever or a zero cash flow. The discount rate is 5 percent. If the initial cost is $10, what is the NPV with the option to stop after the first year?

    A. −$10

    B. $0

    C. $10

    D. $20

4. In the event tree used in the binomial approach to option valuation, at each node the value either increases or decreases by the proportion u or d, respectively. If the standard deviation is 10 percent per year and the horizon is six months, what are the up-movement u and down-movement d values?

    A. 1.0488 and 0.9534

    B. 1.0513 and 0.9511

    C. 1.0733 and 0.9317

    D. 1.2505 and 0.8000

5. In a project where there is an option to proceed after the results of trials, it can be argued that the flexibility to defer the investment decision until trial results are known reduces risk because the adverse outcome of a loss can be avoided. But to correctly value the flexibility in a DTA approach, the discount rate can be higher than the discount rate without flexibility. Explain how lower risk can lead to a higher discount rate.

6. Explain why a change in interest rates can produce either an increase or a decrease in the value of a project with flexibility.

    A. Increase in value because: _____

    B. Decrease in value because: _____

7. To recognize opportunities for creating value from flexibility when assessing investment projects or strategies, managers should ask the following three questions concerning three important details.

A. _____

B. _____

C. _____

8. Outline the four-step process for valuing flexibility.

A. _____

_____

B. _____

_____

C. _____

_____

D. _____

_____

9. A project costs $500 to start and has a 10 percent chance of generating $400 per year forever and a 90 percent chance of generating $50 per year forever. The discount rate is 25 percent. In one year, the investor has the right to expand and start eight more similar projects. What is the NPV with and without the option to expand?

10. A product will have a NPV equal to $4,000 if successful in two years. There is a 20 percent chance it will pass the research phase, which will be determined after the first year, and a 50 percent chance it will pass the testing phase at the end of the second year. The initial costs for getting the research phase started are $240. If it passes the research phase, there will be a required investment of $100. If it passes the testing phase, there will be a required investment of $200. The discount rate for the project is 20 percent and the risk-free rate is 4 percent. Compute the standard NPV and the NPV including the flexibility.

33

Valuation in
Emerging Markets

Valuation is usually difficult in emerging markets because of unique risks and obstacles not present in developed markets. Additional considerations include macroeconomic uncertainty, illiquid capital markets, controls on the flow of capital into and out of the country, less rigorous standards of accounting and disclosure, and high levels of political risk. To estimate value in this environment, an analyst should use a triangulation approach based on values derived from three different methods: (1) a discounted cash flow (DCF) approach with probability-weighted scenarios that model the risks the business faces, (2) a DCF valuation with a country risk premium built into the cost of capital, and (3) a valuation based on comparable trading and transaction multiples.

The DCF approach is basically the same as that for a developed nation with additional steps. As in the case of developed nations, the analyst must develop consistent economic assumptions, forecast cash flows, and compute a WACC. Computing cash flows, however, may require extra work because of accounting differences. If done correctly, the two DCF methods should give the same estimate of value.

1. Match the items on the right to those on the left concerning an emerging market (there is an extra item on the right).

Country risk premium	_____	A. U.S. Treasury bonds plus inflation difference
Risk-free rate	_____	
A reason share price is below intrinsic value	_____	B. The multiples approach
		C. Scenario DCF approach
Recommended primary method for determining value	_____	D. A global market index
		E. Small free float
Recommended input for computing beta	_____	F. The spread of the local government debt rate denominated in U.S. dollars and a U.S. government bond of similar maturity

2. In a two-scenario model of an emerging market, it is recommended that the analyst create a base-case set of forecasts and a set of forecasts associated with a period of economic distress. What range of probability weights is recommended to use for the economic distress scenario? Based on what evidence?

3. Although the cost of capital in emerging markets should be fairly close to a global cost of capital adjusted for local inflation and capital structure, there are five general guidelines to keep in mind. List those guidelines.

A. _____

B. _____

C. _____

D. _____

E. _____

4. Bill Smith and Jan Brown are analysts who are attempting to evaluate a company in an emerging market. Smith recommends creating one integrated set of economic and monetary assumptions and that they should spend extra effort to create the right forecasts. He lists the variables to be included in those assumptions. Brown cautions that the goal should not be to create the right forecasts and suggests a better approach.

A. List the variables for which Smith would most likely wish to create assumptions.

B. Instead of creating the right forecasts, what might Brown be recommending?

C. To what extent should purchasing power parity (PPP) be an element in the forecasts of a company in an emerging market?

5. Given the following information, estimate the value of the company. The cash for the next year is estimated to be either $500 in the business-as-usual scenario or $200 in the distress scenario. The probabilities of the scenarios are 80 percent and 20 percent, respectively. The expected growth rate in each case is 4 percent per year, and the cost of capital is 9 percent.

6. Estimate a country risk premium that is consistent with your answer in Question 5.

34

Valuing High-Growth
Companies

The recommended, standard valuation principles apply to high-growth companies as well; however, there is a difference in the order of the steps of the valuation process and the emphasis on each step. The analyst should forecast the development of the company's markets and then work backward. As in the case of emerging markets, the analyst should create scenarios concerning the market's possible paths of development.

When looking into the future, the analyst should also estimate a point in time at which the company's performance is likely to stabilize and then work backward from that point. By then, the company will have captured a stable market share; and one part of the forecasting process requires determining the size of the market and the company's share. Then, the firm must estimate the inputs for return: operating margins, required capital investments, and ROIC. Finally, the analyst should develop scenarios and apply to the scenarios a set of probability weights consistent with long-term historical evidence on corporate growth.

1. The future state should be defined and bounded by measures of operating performance. List three examples of those measures of operating performance.

A. _____

B. _____

C. _____

2. List three possible methods for dealing with the uncertainty of high-growth companies. Indicate which method the text recommends and the reason why.

A. _____

B. _____

C. _____

3. How should scenario weights be composed and calibrated?

4. How could scenario analysis be employed to gain a better understanding of the value drivers embedded in a high-growth firm?

5. Identify the key issues an analyst should consider when valuing start-up companies. How might an analyst resolve these issues?

6. An analyst computes the intrinsic values and probabilities for each of the indicated scenarios in the following table. Determine the expected intrinsic value and the value per share.

Scenario	Intrinsic value ($ million)	Probability	Intrinsic value x probability
Success in both domestic and international markets	$2,500	0.3	
Success in domestic market	1,500	0.5	
Failure in domestic market	700	0.2	
Expected intrinsic value			
Shares outstanding: 200 million	Expected share price		

7. Referring to the previous question, suppose it is determined that the probability in the first, favorable scenario was too high, and the probability in the least favorable scenario was too low. The revised probabilities are 20 and 30 percent, respectively. Compute the new expected intrinsic value and value per share. What is the percent change in share price, and what does this say about the importance of scenario weights?

Scenario	Intrinsic value ($ million)	Probability	Intrinsic value x probability
Success in both domestic and international markets	$2,500	0.2	
Success in domestic market	1,500	0.5	
Failure in domestic market	700	0.3	
Expected intrinsic value			
Shares outstanding: 200 million	Expected share price		

35

Valuing Cyclical
Companies

A cyclical company is one whose earnings demonstrate a repeating pattern of increases and decreases. The earnings of such companies fluctuate because of large changes in the prices of their products or changes in volume. Volatile earnings introduce additional complexity into the valuation process, as historical performance must be assessed in the context of the cycle.

Although the share prices of companies with cyclical earnings tend to be more volatile than those of less cyclical companies, their discounted cash flow (DCF) valuations are much more stable. Earnings forecasts may be the reason that the former is more volatile than the latter. Analysts' projections of the profits of cyclical companies are not very accurate in that they tend not to forecast the downturns and generally have positive biases. Analysts may produce biased forecasts for these cyclical firms from fear of retaliation from the managers of the firms they analyze.

The behavior of managers may play a role in the cyclicality. They tend to increase and decrease investments at the same time (i.e., exhibit herd behavior). Three explanations for this behavior are (1) cash is generally more available when prices are high, (2) it is easier to get approval from boards of directors for investments when profits are high, and (3) executives get concerned about the possibilities of rivals growing faster than their firms.

The following steps outline one approach for evaluating a cyclical firm: (1) construct and value the normal cycle scenario using information about past cycles; (2) construct and value a new trend line scenario based on the recent performance of the company; (3) develop the economic rationale for each of the two scenarios, considering factors such as demand growth, companies entering or exiting the industry, and technology changes that will affect the balance of supply and demand; and (4) assign probabilities to the scenarios and calculate their weighted values.

1. A firm's free cash flows follow a four-year cycle. In the current year FCF_0 = 10. In each of the next three years FCF will be 20, 40, and 30, and the cycle begins again with 10, 20, and so on in perpetuity. If the discount rate is 10 percent, calculate the present value (PV) of the infinite series of FCFs for each year beginning with the present period and for the next three periods. Compute the (population) standard deviation of both the FCFs and the present values of the FCFs over the four-year cycle.

2. Simulations of capital expenditure timing have shown that the internal rates of return (IRRs) will be different for each of the following patterns. Rank them by placing 1, 2, 3, and 4 in the blanks to indicate which patterns exhibit the highest to lowest IRR.

   A. Spending evenly over cycle: _____

   B. Optimally timed asset purchases: _____

   C. Optimally timed capital spending: _____

   D. Typical spending pattern: _____

3. The point of the results in Exhibit 35.5 in the text is to illustrate how prices indicate that analysts:

   A. Make naive, random-walk forecasts, which are not very accurate.

   B. Make forecasts based on an extrapolation of recent trends.

   C. Make forecasts based on a 50/50 chance the firm will exhibit past cyclicality or break into a new trend.

   D. Should make naive, random-walk forecasts because they would beat most experts.

4. A pessimistic forecast from an analyst may damage the relationships of the analyst with which of the following?

   A. The analyst's employer.

   B. Investment banks.

   C. The managers of the analyzed firm.

   D. All of these.

5. Follow the four steps of the two-scenario approach to estimate the value of a firm given the data for the past few years.

Financial data input	2006	2007	2008	2009	2010
Current assets	2,595	2,615	2,916	2,645	4,559
Current liabilities	1,764	2,490	3,020	2,648	4,191
Debt in current liabilities	0	0	0	0	0
Long-term debt	7,052	6,817	6,460	6,928	8,831
Total assets	12,335	12,818	12,950	12,700	16,897
Capital expenditures	1,503	1,564	892	951	2,609
Change in deferred taxes	10	14	100	38	73
Sales	14,313	13,024	13,094	13,342	17,977
Operating expenses	9,794	9,798	10,209	10,231	13,333
General expenses	1,406	1,475	1,296	1,204	1,670
Depreciation	984	996	1,017	997	1,013

A. First, produce invested capital, NOPLAT, free cash flow, and economic profit statements as well as a return on invested capital (ROIC) value tree to examine the company's cyclical character. Develop a normal scenario value for the company. Here are templates for the statements and ROIC value tree:

	2006	2007	2008	2009	2010
Invested capital statement					
Working capital					
Long-term assets					
Operating invested capital					
Net investment					
Debt					
Equity					
NOPLAT statement					
Sales					
Operating expense					
General expense					
Depreciation					
EBIT					

	2006	2007	2008	2009	2010
Taxes on EBIT					
Change in deferred taxes					
NOPLAT					
Provision for income taxes					
Tax shield on interest expense					
Tax on investment income					
Tax on nonoperating income					
Taxes on EBIT					
Net income statement					
Sales					
Operating expense					
General expense					
Depreciation					
EBIT					
Investment income					
Investment expense					
Miscellaneous, net					
Earnings before taxes					
Income taxes					
Net income (before extra items)					
Tax rate					
Reconciliation to net income statement					
Net income					
Add: Increase in deferred taxes					
Adjusted net income					
Add: Interest expense after tax					
Income available to investors					
Less: Interest income after tax					

(Continued)

(Continued)

	2006	2007	2008	2009	2010
Less: Nonop. income after tax					
NOPLAT					
ROIC tree					
ROIC					
$= (1 -$ EBIT cash tax rate)					
$\times$ Pretax ROIC					
$=$ EBIT/sales					
$\times$ Sales/invested capital					
EBIT/sales $= 1 -$ (Operating expense/sales					
$+$ General expense/sales					
$+$ Depreciation/sales)					
Sales/invested capital					
$= 1/$(Op. working capital/sales					
$+$ Long-term op. assets/sales)					
Change in deferred tax/sales					
Free cash flow statement					
NOPLAT					
Depreciation					
Gross cash flow					
Increase in op. working capital					
Capital expenditures					
Gross investment					
Free cash flow					
Nonoperating cash flow					
Cash flow available to investors					
Cost of capital					
Beta					
Debt/invested capital					
Equity/invested capital					

	2006	2007	2008	2009	2010
Cost of debt					
Cost of equity					
Weighted average cost of capital					
Economic profit					
NOPLAT					
Capital charge					
Economic profit					

Value the normal scenario using the following templates:

	Average 2006–2010	FY 2011	FY 2012	FY 2013	CV 2014
Working capital					
Net fixed assets					
Invested capital					
Net investment					
Debt					
Equity					
Sales growth		4.66%	4.66%	4.66%	
Net sales	14,350,000				
Operating expense					
General expense					
Depreciation					
EBIT					
Taxes on EBIT					
Change in deferred tax					
Net op. profit less adjusted tax					
Net investment					

(*Continued*)

(Continued)

	Average 2006–2010	FY 2011	FY 2012	FY 2013	CV 2014
Free cash flow					
Cost of capital					
Economic profit					
Beta	1.37				
Unlevered beta					
PV factors					
PV sums					
PV short-term forecast					
Continuing value					
PV continuing value					
Market value of assets					
Debt					
Market value of equity					
Number of shares					
Stock price					
Sum					
PV economic profit 1–3					
Continuing value					
PV continuing value					
Invested capital					
Market value of assets					
ROIC					
Debt/invested capital	67.34%	67.34%	67.34%	67.34%	67.34%
Equity/invested capital					
Tax rate	38.71%	38.71%	38.71%	38.71%	38.71%
Interest rate	6.83%	6.83%	6.83%	6.83%	6.83%

	Average 2006–2010	FY 2011	FY 2012	FY 2013	CV 2014
Growth (investment/capital)		4.66%	4.66%	4.66%	4.66%
Investment rate (growth/ROIC)					
EBIT/sales					
Sales/invested capital					
Working capital/sales					
NFAOA/sales					
Operating expense/sales					
SG&A/sales					
Depreciation/sales					
Change in deferred tax/sales					

B. Formulate a new-trend scenario using the following pulp and paper industry data:

Five-year sales growth	6%
Beta	1.01
Operating expenses/sales	70%

Value the new trend scenario using the following template:

	Average 2006–2010	FY 2011	FY 2012	FY 2013	CV 2014
Working capital					
Net fixed assets					
Invested capital					
Net investment					
Debt					

(Continued)

(*Continued*)

	Average 2006–2010	FY 2011	FY 2012	FY 2013	CV 2014
Equity					
Sales growth		6.00%	6.00%	6.00%	
Net sales	14,350,000				
Operating expense					
General expense					
Depreciation					
EBIT					
Taxes on EBIT					
Change in deferred tax					
Net op. profit less adj. tax					
Net investment					
Free cash flow					
Cost of capital					
Economic profit					
Beta	1.37				
Unlevered beta					
PV factors					

	PV sums
PV short-term forecast	
Continuing value	
PV continuing value	
Market value of assets	
Debt	
Market value of equity	
Number of shares	
Stock price	

	Sum
PV economic profit 1–3	578,975
Continuing value	

	Average 2006–2010	FY 2011	FY 2012	FY 2013	CV 2014
PV continuing value	6,780,219				
Invested capital	10,717,400				
Market value of assets					
ROIC					
Debt/invested capital	67.34%	67.34%	67.34%	67.34%	67.34%
Equity/invested capital					
Tax rate	38.71%	38.71%	38.71%	38.71%	38.71%
Interest rate	6.83%	6.83%	6.83%	6.83%	6.83%
Growth (investment/capital)		6.00%	6.00%	6.00%	4.66%
Investment rate (growth/ROIC)					
EBIT/sales					
Sales/invested capital					
Working capital/sales					
NFAOA/sales					
Operating expense/sales					
SG&A/sales					
Depreciation/sales					
Change in deferred tax/sales					

36

Valuing Banks

There are three complications in the valuation of banks: the latitude managers have with respect to accounting decisions, the level of leverage, and the fact that banks are multibusiness companies. Those businesses include borrowing and lending, underwriting and placement of securities, payment services, asset management, proprietary trading, and brokerage.

In valuing a bank, the discounted cash flow (DCF) on operations approach is not appropriate because interest rates revenue and costs are part of operating income. The equity DCF method is more appropriate, and the analyst should triangulate the results with a multiples-based valuation. The equity approach uses a modified version of the value driver formula in which return on equity (ROE) and return on new equity (RONE) replace ROIC and RONIC, and net income replaces NOPLAT:

$$CV = \frac{NI\left(1 - \dfrac{g}{RONE}\right)}{k - g}$$

Problems associated with applying the equity DCF valuation method include determining the source of value, the effect of leverage, and the cost of holding equity capital. Economic spread analysis can help determine the sources of value creation. Other complications in bank valuations are monitoring the yield curve and forward rates, estimating loan loss provisions, approximating the bank's equity risk capital needs, and constructing separate statements for each of the bank's activities.

1. Which of the following best describes maturity mismatch and its role in bank operations?

    A. It refers to banks selling old loans so they can take on new loans, which earns a capital gain.

    B. It refers to banks lending long-term and borrowing short-term, which earns positive net interest income.

    C. It refers to the outdated accounting rules that most banks must operate under.

    D. It refers to the inequality between accounting allowances for bad loans and the actual rate of losses on those loans.

2. Which of the following will change the cost of equity?

    I. Asset composition.

    II. Liability composition.

    III. The expected market return.

    IV. The risk-free rate.

     A. I and II only.

     B. I, III, and IV only.

     C. III and IV only.

     D. I, II, III, and IV.

3. The best method for understanding how much value a bank is creating in its different product lines is:

    A. Free cash flow analysis.

    B. Ratio analysis.

    C. Economic spread analysis.

    D. Net income analysis.

4. Which of the following is the usual ordering of the absolute value of the types of loan losses to banks?

    A. Credit card losses > mortgage losses > business loan losses.

    B. Mortgage losses > business loan losses > credit card losses.

    C. Credit card losses > business loan losses > mortgage losses.

    D. Mortgage losses > credit card losses > business loan losses.

5. In the following list, identify whether the term relates to trading income or other income. Write "Trading" or "Other," respectively.

    A. Real estate: _____

    B. Foreign exchange: _____

C. Minority investments: _____

D. Pension products: _____

E. Bonds: _____

F. Credit default swaps: _____

G. Asset-backed obligations: _____

6. Based on Exhibit 36.1 in the text, rank the sources of income for European banks from largest (1) to smallest (4). Indicate rankings for both 1988 and 2007. How have the relative sizes (as opposed to the rankings) changed?

	1988	2007
Commission income	_____	_____
Interest income	_____	_____
Trading income	_____	_____
Other	_____	_____

7. The following information is a simplified balance sheet of a bank. The relevant yields are 10 percent on loans, 2 percent on deposits, and a 4 percent intercompany interest rate on reserves for the spread model. Apply the latter rate to reserves and equity. The tax rate is 40 percent and other expenses are $30.

Assets		Liabilities	
Cash reserves	$130	Deposits	$760
Loans	670	Equity	40
Total assets	800		

A. Calculate the net income with the income model:

Interest income

Interest expense

Other expenses   _____

Net profit before taxes

Taxes   _____

Net income

B. Calculate net income with the spread model:

Loan spread	
Deposit spread	
Equity spread	
Reserve debt	
Expenses	_____
Net profit before taxes	
Taxes	_____
Net income	

C. Compare the two models and demonstrate why they produce the same net income in this case.

8. The following is a set of forecasts of a bank for net income, changes in equity, and other comprehensive income or loss. The period 2011–2015 is the explicit forecast period. In the early years the bank forecasts that it will have to raise new equity to lift its Tier 1 ratio from 3 to 6 percent, which will produce large decreases in equity. This will stabilize in 2014 and remain at a negative 11 in the foreseeable future. The other comprehensive income will remain at 2 in perpetuity beyond year 2014, too. Net income will be 90 in 2016 and is expected to grow at 2 percent thereafter. The return on new equity will be 10 percent. The required return on equity is 8 percent. Compute the present value of the forecasted cash flows.

Cash flow statement forecasts	2011	2012	2013	2014	2015
Net income	73	77	81	85	88
Increase or decrease in equity	−90	−90	−10	−11	−11
Other comprehensive income or loss	−1	0	1	2	2
Cash flow to equity					
				$CV_{2015} =$	
Cash flow value					
PV(CFE) =					

Part Two

Answers

Why Value Value?

1. Data from both Europe and the United States found that the correlation between value creation and employment in the company has been *positive* and *significant*.

2. In the past 30 years there have been at least *six* financial crises that arose largely because companies and banks were *financing illiquid assets with short-term debt*.

3. Two activities that managers often use in an attempt to increase share price but that do not actually create value are changes in *capital structure* and changes in *accounting practices*.

4. The conservation of value corollary of the value creation principle says that *anything that does not increase cash flows* does not create value.

5. During the Internet boom of the late 1990s, the Microsoft model did not work for many firms because they blindly pursued *getting bigger* without *maintaining a competitive advantage*.

6. B

7. D

8. A

9. C

10. D

2

Fundamental Principles of
Value Creation

1.

Types of growth	Ranking
A. Increase share in a growing market.	1. D
B. Expand an existing market.	2. B
C. Acquire businesses.	3. A
D. Introduce new products to market.	4. C

2. The firm should engage in share repurchases only if it does not have available investments with sufficiently high ROIC.

3. Financial engineering is the use of financial instruments or structures, other than straight debt and equity, to manage a company's capital structure and risk profile.

4. Earnings and cash flow are often *correlated*, but earnings don't tell the whole story of value creation, and focusing too much on earnings or earnings growth *can lead to straying away from the value-creating path*.

5. When ROIC is greater than the cost of capital, the relationship between growth and value is *positive*. When ROIC is less than the cost of capital, the relationship between growth and value is *negative*. When ROIC equals the cost of capital, the relationship between growth and value is *zero*.

6. With respect to countries, the core valuation principle is *applicable*, as made evident by the fact that U.S. companies trade *at higher multiples than* companies in other countries.

7. When comparing the effect of an increase in growth on a high-ROIC company and a low-ROIC company, a 1 percent increase in growth will have *a higher positive effect on the high-ROIC company.*

8. Because interest expense is tax deductible, share repurchases can have the beneficial effect of *increasing earnings per share*, but this may not increase share price because *the price-to-earnings (P/E) ratio may decline.*

9. D

10. D. Investment rate = Growth/ROIC = 2%/10% = 20%.

11. C

$$\$2500 = \frac{NOPLAT_{t=1} \cdot \left(1 - \dfrac{\text{growth}}{\text{ROIC}}\right)}{\text{WACC} - \text{growth}}$$

$$\$2500 = \frac{\$300 \cdot \left(1 - \dfrac{5\%}{15\%}\right)}{13\% - 5\%}$$

The Expectations Treadmill

Percentage	Traditional	Enhanced
Growth	10.0	10.0
Required investment		(3.3)
TRS from performance		6.7
Zero-growth return		8.3
Change in P/E	5.0	5.0
Dividend yield	5.0	
TRS	20.0	20.0

1. D. TRS from performance $= (E_1/E_0 - 1) - (K_1/K_0 - 1) = (\$22/\$20 - 1) - (\$206.6/\$200 - 1) = 6.7\%$.

2. C. Dividend yield $= (D_1/EV_0) = \$12/\$240 = 5\%$.

3. A. Zero-growth return $= 1/12 = 8.3\%$.

4. D. TRS $= 10\% + 5.0\% + 5.0\% = 20.0\%$.

5. The components in the two-component breakdown are:
   A. Percent change in share price.
   B. Percent change in dividend yield.

The components in the three-component breakdown are:

A. Percent change in earnings.

B. Percent change in P/E.

C. Percent change in dividend yield.

6. For periods of *10* years or more, it is true that if managers focus on *improving TRS to win performance bonuses*, then their interests and the interests of shareholders should be aligned.

7. The detrimental result of the expectations treadmill is that, for firms that have had superior operating and TRS performance, the managers who try to continually meet the higher expectations may engage in detrimental activities such as *ill-advised acquisitions* or *new ventures*.

4

Return on Invested Capital

1. Porter's five forces are:
   A. Threat of entry.
   B. Pressure from substitute products.
   C. Bargaining power of buyers.
   D. Bargaining power of suppliers.
   E. The degree of rivalry among existing competitors.

2. The key driver of ROIC is *competitive advantage.*

3. Companies have been fairly successful in sustaining their rates of ROIC.

4. In the context of competitive advantage and ROIC, quality means a real or perceived difference between one product or service and another that prompts consumers to pay a higher price.

5. For a pricing advantage, using rational pricing discipline requires either a *price leader that all other producers follow* or *barriers to entry.*

6. The two terms (economies of scale and scalable products) are similar, but they are not the same. If a firm has economies of scale, then its average costs decline as output increases. If a firm has scalable products, then its additional costs for producing the product are essentially zero for each additional unit of output. An example is the delivery of physical goods and the delivery of information via the Internet. Physical goods require a cost for delivery, but that cost to a given location would be lower for each

additional unit in a given delivery. In the delivery of information, the first and last unit would have about the same delivery cost, which would be essentially zero.

7. Between 1963 and 2008, the median ROIC was *10* percent and the interquartile range was *5* percent to *20* percent.

8. Compared to the stability of rates of growth, rates of ROIC tend to *remain fairly stable.*

9. Rank of industry based on ROIC:

A. Computers and peripherals	1. B
B. Pharmaceuticals	2. A
C. Paper packaging	3. C

The median ROICs for A, B, and C are about 12 percent, 25 percent, and 8 percent, respectively.

10. B. ROICs tend to be mean reverting, but firms tend to sustain their relative position to the mean (i.e., either higher or lower) for 10 years or more.

11. A. 6.8 percent.

$$\text{ROIC} = (1 - 0.32)\frac{\$3.40 - \$1.80}{\$16} = 0.068$$

12. C. For cereal manufacturers and meat producers, the ROICs are 30 percent and 15 percent, respectively. Cereal manufacturers earn a higher return as a result of being able to brand their products.

5

Growth

1. The two sources of organic growth are (1) portfolio momentum or increase in the size of the market and (2) increasing market share. Market growth explains more than twice the overall growth explained by increasing market share.

2. Incremental innovation will rarely create lasting value, because competitors can easily retaliate. Competitors can either lower the prices on their existing products or, if the innovator raises the price of the improved product, keep their prices the same. Also, the rivals can also come up with their own incremental innovations, which is easier than coming up with a new product or service.

3. With respect to product development. growth is difficult to maintain because for each product *that is maturing and reaching its peak in revenue*, the company must *develop a new product that will grow faster to replace it*. This is called the *treadmill* effect.

4. Publicly traded firms have grown at a higher rate than GDP. The two reasons for this are:
   A. Publicly traded firms can grow faster because of their ease in raising capital, so their growth can be higher than the overall economy at the expense of nonpublic firms.
   B. Public firms have experienced higher growth from expanding sales to overseas markets, and expanding markets and bringing in new consumers are the most effective means of growing and creating value.

5. B

6. A

7. D

8. B

9. A

10. C

6

Frameworks for Valuation

1. Value of the equity = DFCF + Nonoperating assets − Nonequity claims.
   Value of the equity = \$400m + \$9m − \$220m − \$33m = \$156m.
   Value of each share of common stock = \$156m/2m = \$78.

2. Value of the equity = Discounted economic profit + Invested capital + Nonoperating assets − Nonequity claims.
   Value of the equity = \$150m + \$250m + \$16m − \$80m − \$26m.
   Value of each share of common stock = \$310m.

3. C

4. A

5. Economic profit = Invested capital × (ROIC − WACC).
   Economic profit = \$300m × (12% − 10.5%) = \$4.5m.

6. The Modigliani-Miller proposition says that without the effect of taxes, the capital structure should not affect the value of the firm. The adjusted present value model computes the value of the firm as if it were all-equity financed and then adds the value of the debt tax shield.

7.

Source of capital	Proportion of total capital	Cost of capital	Marginal tax rate	After-tax cost of capital	Contribution to WACC
Debt	42%	6.2%	34%	<u>4.09%</u>	1.72%
Equity	58%	9.8%		<u>9.8%</u>	5.68%
WACC					7.40%

8. Since the cash flows and the tax shields will grow at a constant rate, the value of each can be estimated with the constant growth model. Both are discounted using the unlevered cost of equity.

$$V = \$40m/(9\% - 5\%) + \$9m/(9\% - 3\%) = \$1,150m$$

9.

Year	Free cash flow	Interest tax shield	Discount factor	PV of free CF	PV of interest TS
2011	402	31	0.9174	368.8	28.4
2012	420	32	0.8417	353.5	26.9
2013	436	34	0.7722	336.7	26.3
Continuing value	8,900	380	0.7722	6,872.4	293.4
Present value				7,931.4	375.0

PV of free cash flow	7,931.4
PV of interest tax shield	375.0
PV of free cash flow and interest tax shield	8,306.4
Midyear adjustment factor	622
Value of operations	8,928.4
Value of long-term investments	155
Value of tax loss carry-forwards	81
Enterprise value	9,164.4
Value of debt	2,583
Value of capitalized operating leases	1,674
Equity value	4,907.4

7

Reorganizing the Financial Statements

1. A

2. D

3. B

4. B

5. C. $17,857 = \$5,000/(0.08 + 1/5)$.

6. B

7. B

8. Total funds invested = OA − OL + NOA = \$400 − \$60 + \$100 + \$50 = \$490 = D + \$30 + \$200. Debt = \$260.

9. Given the accounting income statement on the left, enter the appropriate entries into the NOPLAT worksheet on the right and compute income available to investors. The marginal tax rate is 30 percent.

Revenues	$2,000	Revenues	$2,000
Operating costs	(1,000)	Operating costs	(1,000)
Depreciation	(400)	Depreciation	(400)
Operating profit	$600	Operating profit	$600
Interest	(40)	Operating taxes	(180)
Nonoperating income	10	NOPLAT	420
Earnings before taxes	$570	After-tax nonoperating income	7
Taxes	(171)	Income available to investors	$427
Net income	$399		

Adding back the after-tax interest expense of $28 = (1 − 0.3) ∗ $40 to net income gives the income available to investors, which shows that the adjustments are correct.

10. NOPLAT = $35.0
 Working capital = $44
 Invested capital = $194
 Total funds invested = $199

NOPLAT	Year	**Total funds invested**	Year
Revenues	200.0	Working cash	10
Cost of sales	(80.0)	Accounts receivable	30
Selling costs	(50.0)	Inventories	10
Depreciation	(20.0)	Accounts payable	(6)
Operating profit	50.0	**Working capital**	44
Operating taxes	(15.0)	Property, plant, and equipment	150
NOPLAT	35.0	**Invested capital**	194
		Prepaid pension assets	5
Reconciliation of NOPLAT		Total funds invested	199
Net income	32.2		
Tax audit	—		
After-tax interest expense	(2.8)	*Reconciliation of total funds invested*	
After-tax gain on sale	—	Short-term debt	12
NOPLAT	35.0	Long-term debt	70
		Restructuring reserves	7
		Debt and debt equivalents	89
		Equity	110
		Total funds invested	199

8

Analyzing Performance and Competitive Position

1. ROE mixes operating performance with capital structure.

   ROA includes nonoperating assets, and it ignores the benefits of accounts payable and other operating liabilities.

2. D

3. C. ROIC $= (1 - 0.25) * (3,000/5,000) * (5,000/20,000) = 11.25\%$.

4. A

5. C

6. C

7. B

8. C

9.

2008	EBIT interest	EBITDA interest	EBITDAR (interest + rental expense)
Numerator	48	187	187
Denominator	39	39	39
Ratio	1.23	4.79	4.79

2009	EBIT interest	EBITDA interest	EBITDAR (interest + rental expense)
Numerator	20	156	404
Denominator	30	30	278
Ratio	0.667	5.20	1.45

10. Days $= 365 \times$ (Cash/revenues).
Cash $=$ Current assets $-$ (Receivables $+$ Inventories $+$ Other current assets).
Cash $= \$863 - \$523 = \$340$.
Days $= 365 \times (\$340/\$4,056) = 30.60$ days.

Forecasting Performance

1. True

2. True

3. False

4. False

5. True

6. B

7. C

8. C

9. C

10. A

11. The problem is that the parent company can record only the dividends received and not the entire cash and revenue received from the investments. The analyst cannot use traditional drivers for these investments, but instead must estimate future nonoperating income by examining historical growth in nonoperating income or by examining the revenue and profit forecasts of publicly traded companies that are comparable to the equity investment.

12. Top-down forecast:
    A. Step 1: Size the whole market.
    B. Step 2: Determine market share.
    C. Step 3: Forecast prices.
    Bottom-up forecast:
    A. Input 1: Estimate demand from existing customers.
    B. Input 2: Estimate customer turnover.
    C. Input 3: Estimate potential for new customers.

13.

Typical Forecast Drivers for the Income Statement

	Line item	Typical forecast driver	Typical forecast ratio
Operating	Cost of goods sold	Revenue	COGS/revenue
	Selling, general, and administrative expense	Revenue	SG&A/revenue
	Depreciation	Prior-year net PP&E	$Depreciation_t$/net $PP\&E_{t-1}$
Nonoperating	Interest expense	Prior-year to total debt	Interest $expense_t$/ total $debt_{t-1}$
	Interest income	Prior-year to excess cash	Interest $income_t$/ excess $cash_{t-1}$

14.

	2009	2010		2009	2010
Revenue growth		20%	Revenues	500	600
Cost of goods sold/ revenue	40%	40%	Cost of goods sold	(200)	(240)
Selling and general expenses/revenues	30%	20%	Selling and general expenses	(150)	(120)
Depreciation/net PP&E	20%	30%	Depreciation	(56)	(100.8)
EBITA/revenues			EBITA	94	139.2
Interest rate					
Interest expense	10%	8%	Interest expense	(40)	(35.2)
Interest income	6%	5%	Interest income	12	10
			Nonoperating income	10	13

(Continued)

(Continued)

	2009	2010		2009	2010
Nonoperating items			Earnings before taxes	76	127
Nonoperating income growth		30%			
			Provision for income taxes	(22.8)	(38.1)
Taxes			Net income	53.2	88.9
Average tax rate	30%	30%			

	2008	2009		2008	2009
Assets			Liabilities and equity		
Operating cash	10	10	Accounts payable	20	24
Excess cash	200	200	Short-term debt	300	330
Inventory	60	72	Current liabilities	320	354
Current assets	270	282			
			Long-term debt	100	110
Net PP&E	280	336	Common stock	80	80
Equity investments	100	100	Retained earnings	150	174
Total assets	650	718	Total liabilities and equity	650	718

Estimating
Continuing Value

1. True

2. False

3. False

4. True

5. False

6. C

7. A

8. A

9. B

10. A

11. A. Multiples: The company will be worth some multiple of book value or price-to-earnings.

B. Liquidation value: The company will be worth the value of proceeds from the sale of assets at the end of the explicit forecast period after paying the liabilities.

C. Replacement cost: The continuing value equals what it would take to purchase the firm's assets at the end of the forecast period.

12.

$$CV_t = \frac{NOPLAT_{t+1}\left[1 - \frac{g}{RONIC}\right]}{WACC - g}$$

$$CV_t = \frac{\$200\left[1 - \frac{0.04}{0.08}\right]}{0.06 - 0.04} = \$5,000$$

13.

$$CV_t = \frac{IC_t\,[ROIC_t - WACC]}{WACC} + \frac{PV\,(Economic\ Profit_{t+2})}{WACC - g}$$

$$PV\,(Economic\ Profit_{t+2}) = \frac{NOPLAT_{t+1}\left[\frac{g}{RONIC}\right](RONIC - WACC)}{WACC}$$

PV(Economic Profit$_{t+2}$) = \$500 × (.02/0.10) × (0.10 − 0.07)/0.07 = \$42.86

$CV_t = \$2,000 \times (0.12 - 0.07)/0.07 + \$42.86/(0.07 - 0.02)$

$CV_t = \$1,428.57 + \$857.20$

$CV_t = \$2,285.77$

14.

	Year 1	Year 2	Year 3	CV	Key value drivers	
Revenues	$200.0	$210.0	$216.0	$220.0	Investment rate	60.0%
Operating costs	(180.0)	(189.0)	(194.4)	(198.0)	Return on new capital	15.0%
Operating margin	$20.0	$21.0	$21.6	$22.0	Growth rate	9.0%
Operating taxes	(6.0)	(6.3)	(6.5)	(6.6)	Operating costs as percent of sales	90.0%
NOPLAT	$14.0	$14.7	$15.1	$15.4	Operating taxes	30.0%
					NOPLAT margin	7.0%
Net investment	(8.4)	(8.8)	(9.1)	CV		
Free cash flow	$5.6	$5.9	$6.0	$183.3		
					ROIC	14.0%

	Year 1	Year 2	Year 3	CV	Key value drivers	
Discounted cash flow					Cost of capital	12.0%
Discount rate	1.120	1.254	1.405	1.405		
Discounted cash flow	$5.0	$4.7	$4.3	$130.5		
Value of operations	$144.49					

11

Estimating the Cost of Capital

1. D

2. B

3. C

4. B

5. A

6. C

7. $R_A = (6\% - 8\% + 0\% + 12\%)/4 = 2.5\%$
   $R_G = (1.06 * 0.92 * 1.0 * 1.12)^{0.25} - 1 = 2.23\%$
   Forecasted annual return $= 2.41\% = 2.5\% * (4 - 2)/(4 - 1) + 2.23\% * (2 - 1)/(4 - 1)$

8. Industry beta $= 0.45 = [(0.7/1.4) + (1.2/3)]/2$
   Equity beta for Firm A $= 0.45 * 1.4 = 0.63$
   Equity beta for Firm B $= 0.45 * 3 = 1.35$

9. WACC $= 0.5 * (10\%) + 0.5 * (6\%) * (1 - 0.4) = 6.8\%$

10. V = (1,500,000 * $10) + (8,000 * $1,125) = $24,000,000
    The weights are
    E/V = 15,000,000/24,000,000 = 0.625
    D/V = 9,000,000/24,000,000 = 0.375
    WACC = 0.625 * 12% + 0.375 * 9% * (1 − 0.34) = 9.73%

Moving from Enterprise Value to Value per Share

1. B

2. A

3. C

4. B

5. D

6. D

7. In order of listing,

$$\text{Value of the firm} = \$320m + \$25m - \$2m - \$185m + \$2m - \$4m - \$6m$$
$$= \$150m$$

Value per share = $150m/(2m shares) = $75/share

8.

Excess real estate	+
Preferred stock	−
Minority interest	−
Tax loss carry-forward	+
Unfunded pension liabilities	−
Nonconsolidated subsidiaries	+

9. Is book value a reasonable approximation for evaluating the asset or liability?

   A. Yes

   B. No

   C. Yes

   D. No

   E. No

   F. Yes

   G. No

   H. No

10. A. The subsidiary is not publicly traded, and the stake is less than 20 percent of the value of the subsidiary.

   B. The tracking portfolio method.

13

Calculating and Interpreting Results

1. C

2. C

3. B

4. A

5. C

6. A. Unadjusted financial statements: The balance sheet should balance each year, and the dividends and retained earnings should be congruous with net income.

   B. Rearranged financial statements: The sum of invested capital plus non-operating assets equals the cumulative sources of financing. NOPLAT is the same when calculated from the top down or from the bottom up.

   C. Statement of cash flows: The excess cash and debt line up with the cash flow statement.

7. A. The sensitivity of the results to broad economic conditions.

   B. The level of competitiveness of the industry.

   C. The internal capabilities of the company to achieve the forecasts of output and growth.

   D. The ability of the company to raise the necessary capital from the markets.

8. Three examples of trade-offs are:

A. Sales and prices.

B. Lower inventory and higher sales.

C. Higher growth and lower margin.

9.

	Year 1	Year 2	Year 3
Number of units	200	220	242
Price per unit	$100	$104	$110
Cost per unit	$90	$90	$90
Income	$2,000	$3,080	$4,840
Invested capital	$20,000	$21,000	$22,540
ROIC	10.00%	14.67%	21.47%

These results are not realistic for a competitive industry because the ROIC becomes too high. It is likely that competitors would enter the market and lower sales and/or depress prices.

10. A.

	Year 1	Year 2	Year 3
Number of units	200	220	242
Price per unit	$100	$104	$110
Cost per unit	$90	$93.6	$99
Net income	$2,000	$2,288	$2,662
Invested capital	$20,000	$21,000	$22,144
ROIC	10.00%	10.90%	12.02%

B.

	Year 1	Year 2	Year 3
Number of units	200	200	200
Price per unit	$100	$104	$110
Cost per unit	$90	$90	$90
Net income	$2,000	$2,800	$4,000
Invested capital	$20,000	$21,000	$22,400
ROIC	10.00%	13.33%	17.86%

11. Based on these results, the constant costs assumption seems to be responsible for the high ROIC. When costs increase with inflation, the ROIC increases to only 12.02 percent.

Using Multiples to
Triangulate Results

1. C

2. A

3. C

4. A

5. Adjusted PEG ratio $= 4.5/(100 * .03) = 1.5$.

6.
$$\frac{\text{Value}}{\text{EBITA}} = \frac{(1-\text{T})\left(1 - \frac{g}{\text{ROIC}}\right)}{\text{WACC} - g} = \frac{(1-0.34)\left(1 - \frac{0.04}{0.10}\right)}{0.09 - 0.04} = 7.92$$

7. The measure should remove cash from the invested capital and the interest from the revenues. Since the interest is a pretax cost, this means that revenues will decline by $\$2.40 = \$200 * 0.02 * (1-0.4)$ so that ROIC $= 18.45$ percent $= \$147.60/\$800$.

$$\frac{\text{Value}}{\text{EBITA}} = \frac{(1-\text{T})\left(1 - \frac{g}{\text{ROIC}}\right)}{\text{WACC} - g} = \frac{(1-0.40)\left(1 - \frac{0.05}{0.1845}\right)}{0.10 - 0.05} = 8.75$$

8. A. Production methodology: capital intensive versus capital light.

   B. Distribution channels: online versus bricks and mortar.

   C. Research and development: internal versus acquired.

9. A. EBITA is superior to EBIT because amortization is a measure determined by past acquisitions. It does not affect future cash flows, and therefore it should not be included in the operating earnings measure.

   B. EBITA is superior to EBITDA because the earnings measure should include depreciation. Although analysts often exclude depreciation because it is a noncash measure reflecting past cash outflows, depreciation is important in this case because it gives an indication of what will have to be invested in the future to replace the existing assets.

10. Examples of nonfinancial ratios include ratios of value to web site hits, value to unique visitors, and value to number of subscribers. These measures had some explanatory power for prices in the early years of the wave of Internet companies. After the industry matured, they lost power relative to the explanatory power of gross profit and R&D spending.

15

Market Value Tracks Return on Invested Capital and Growth

1. C

2. C

3. D

4. C

5. B

6. C

7. D

8. B

9.

1960–1968: D   A. TRS averaged 5 percent and was very volatile.

1968–1982: E   B. Interest rates and inflation fell, and TRS was more than

1982–1996: B   16 percent.

1996–2004: A   C. TRS averaged –5 percent per year and was very volatile.

2004–2008: C   D. There was low inflation and an average TRS per year of 9 percent.

E. Inflation increased and TRS averaged –1 percent per year.

10.

$$\text{Expected return} = \frac{E}{P} \times \left(1 - \frac{g}{\text{ROE}}\right) + g = \frac{1}{20} \times \left(1 - \frac{5\%}{25\%}\right) + 5\% = 9\%$$

Markets Value Substance,
Not Form

1. B

2. A

3. D

4. B

5. A

6. B

7. C

8. C

9. D

10. A

11. A. Managers may attempt to lead analysts to adjust their earnings forecasts over time and in a controlled manner by gradually providing new information. This has not been found to affect share price.

B. Managers use accounting adjustments, such as when costs or revenues are recognized, and capitalize costs and R&D. This has not been found to affect share price.

C. Managers make business decisions such as reducing expenditures on advertising, providing customer incentives that do not have immediate costs, and deferring divestments. This can affect share price if the decision destroys value, which such actions often do.

17

Emotions and Mispricing in the Market

1. False

2. True

3. True

4. False

5. False

6. False

7. True

8. True

9. True

10. True

11. A

12. B

13. C

14. C

15. A

16. Network effects are similar to increasing returns to scale. The concept refers to a company making its product the dominant product in a market sector and then introducing other products that directly tie into the first product. Thus, the new products have an advantage over other products in that they either support the original product, which is already pervasive in the market, or need the original product for support. A good example of this is Microsoft's operating system. Once it became the dominant operating system, Microsoft could introduce products that were dependent upon the system (e.g., Excel), which would then have a market advantage over other such software that did not use Microsoft's operating system. Misapplication of the concept helped fuel the Internet bubble. Other firms attempted to put Microsoft's model into place in other industries, e.g., mobile-phone service providers, and investors thought fast growth necessarily led to high profits. Stock prices rose to reflect expectations of Microsoft's level of success in other firms. The other industries did not have the barriers to entry that Microsoft enjoyed, and as competition increased, the stock prices eventually fell.

18

Investors and Managers in Efficient Markets

1. D

2. C

3. A

4. A

5. B

6. D

7. B

8.

Type of investor	Number of positions	Total trading per year per investment	Effective trading per day	Total trading per year per segment
Intrinsic	L	M	H	L
Trader	M	H	L	H
Mechanical	H	L	M	M

9.

Intrinsic: C	A. Seeks profits by betting on short-term movements.
Trader: A	B. Makes decisions based on strict criteria.
Mechanical: B	C. Scrutinizes investments for a month or more before taking positions.

10. Managers need to know their investor base so they can communicate their company's strategy for value creation effectively to different investor segments.

19

Corporate Portfolio Strategy

1. A. *Unique links with other businesses* include distribution lines, access to research and development, and manufacturing advantages.

   B. *Distinctive skills* include means of advertising and managing certain types of businesses.

   C. *Better governance* leads to more fruitful interaction between owners and managers.

   D. *Better insight and foresight* lead to following trends in the early years to benefit from the potential growth and recognizing budding needs in companies and consumers.

   E. *Influence on critical stakeholders* is usually more important in emerging markets, and it refers to having access to key individuals in government or who can influence markets when the markets are not efficient.

2.   i. D and possibly A and C

     ii. C

     iii. D and possibly A and C

     iv. A and possibly D

     v. B

     vi. C

     vii. A

3. i. D
   ii. F
  iii. A
   iv. E
    v. B

     C does not belong on the list.

4. A. Ennerall: Conglom offered capital and links with other businesses. It may have offered manufacturing advantages.

     Corwin Company: Conglom offered managerial skills, a distribution network, and marketing and sales synergies.

  B. Conglom should divest Ennerall. Conglom is probably not in a good position to help Ennerall develop new products. Conglom helped boost sales via its distribution network in drugstores, but now those advantages are over. Ennerall's managers are making large investments, which may not pay off.

20

Performance Management

1. C

2. D

3. C

4. D

5. C

6. Sustain or improve it.

7. A key issue concerning accurately assessing a company's recent strong growth is to determine if it came at the expense of long-term growth.

8. Key value drivers should allow management to articulate how the organization's strategy creates value.

9. Diagnostics of organizational health typically measure:
    A. The skills and capabilities of the company.
    B. Its ability to retain its employees and keep them satisfied.
    C. Its culture and values.
    D. The depth of management talent.

10. A. Medium-term
    B. Short-term
    C. Medium-term
    D. Long-term
    E. Short-term
    F. Short-term
    G. Medium-term

11. A range of targets is a better system, in which there is a base target and a stretch target. The base target is set by top management and is based on prior-year performance and the competitive environment. It is one that managers should meet under any circumstances, and not meeting this target might mean the managers would lose their jobs. The stretch target is an aspiration set by the managers responsible for delivering the target, and there should be a reward for achieving it but no penalty for not achieving it.

21

Mergers and Acquisitions

1. B

2. D

3. A

4. D

5. C

6. A

7. Three market conditions that have led to an increase in acquisitions:
   A. High stock prices.
   B. Low interest rates.
   C. A recent large acquisition in the industry.

8. A. Archetypical
   B. Archetypical
   C. Difficult
   D. Archetypical
   E. Difficult
   F. Archetypical
   G. Difficult

H. Difficult

I. Archetypical

9. In the case of borrowing cash for the acquisition, EPS will probably go up because the after-tax cost of debt might be low relative to the return on assets of the acquisition. The cash acquisition can destroy value for the acquiring shareholders, however, if the increase in leverage increases risk, and that increase is relatively high compared to the revenue increase from the target.

10. Many managers focus on the accretion and dilution of earnings from the acquisition rather than the value it could create. This is why many managers often choose cash for the acquisition. However, stock markets do not pay attention to the effects of an acquisition on accounting numbers.

11.

Function	Examples
1. Research and development	i. Stopping redundant projects.
	ii. Elimination of overlap in research personnel.
	iii. Development of new products through transferred technology.
2. Procurement	i. Pooled purchasing.
	ii. Standardizing products.
3. Manufacturing	i. Elimination of overcapacity.
	ii. Transferring best operating practices.
4. Sales and marketing	i. Cross-selling products.
	ii. Use of common channels.
	iii. Transferring best practices.
	iv. Lowering combined marketing budget.
5. Distribution	i. Consolidated warehouses.
	ii. Consolidated transportation routes.
6. Administration	i. Economies of scale.
	ii. Consolidation of strategy and leadership functions.

12. The value of the new firm will be $102 billion, so the acquiring firm's shareholders get a 2 percent return: $0.02 = (102 - 100)/100$, but the target firm's shareholders reap a return of 33 percent: $0.33 = (8 - 6)/6$.

22

Creating Value
through Divestitures

1. True

2. False

3. True

4. True

5. True

6. False

7. True

8. True

9. False

10. True

11. A

12. A

13. B

14. B

15. C

16.

Type of divestiture	Public or private?	Definition (letter from list)
Trade sale	Private	D
Spin-off	Public	C
Split-off	Public	G
Carve-out	Public	B
IPO	Public	F
Joint venture	Private	A

E does not belong on the list.

23

Capital Structure

1. A. Higher
   B. Higher
   C. Lower
   D. Higher
   E. Higher
   F. Lower
   G. Lower
   H. Higher

2. A. Internal funds
   B. Debt
   C. Equity
   The evidence does not support this ordering of choices. According to the pecking-order theory, mature, profitable firms will have lower leverage; however, large firms generating large cash flows are usually the most highly leveraged.

3. BBB (highest), A, BB, AAA (lowest).

4. C, A, then B.

5. The market-based ratings approach uses option theory to assess the market's evaluation of the equity as a claim on the assets of the firm after paying the strike price, which is the value of the debt. It may be superior

because it uses the collective intelligence of market participants rather than the analytical tools of a rating agency. Also, rating agencies may be slow in making ratings changes, and the market-based approach can make an assessment based on day-to-day changes in the fundamentals of the firm.

6. A. +
   B. +
   C. −
   D. +
   E. +
   F. −
   G. − (Generally negative but can be positive for a firm in distress.)
   H. +

7. Conditions that justify use of derivatives to hedge risk:
   A. The risks are clearly defined.
   B. The derivatives are reasonably priced.
   C. The total risk exposures are large enough so that they could harm the firm's health.

8. A. Convertible debt makes sense when investors or lenders differ from managers in their assessment of the company's credit risk. When the discrepancy is great, it may become difficult to achieve agreement on the terms of credit.
   B. High-growth companies tend to use more convertible debt because convertible debt is less sensitive to differences in credit risk assessment and can facilitate agreement on debt terms. Such differences in assessments are more likely for a high-growth company.

9. The enterprise value initially increases as leverage increases due to:
   A. Tax savings.
   B. Reduction in overinvestment.
   The enterprise value decreases as leverage increases beyond a given point due to:
   A. The cost of business erosion.
   B. Investor conflicts.

10. Although academics argue that every corporation has an optimal capital structure, most surveys among financial executives show that executives put more emphasis on preserving financial flexibility than on minimizing

the cost of capital. Empirical analyses have demonstrated that companies actively manage their capital structures and stay within certain leverage boundaries. Companies are much more likely to issue equity when they are overleveraged relative to this target, and much less likely when they are underleveraged. Companies typically make adjustments toward a target capital structure with one or two years' delay, rather than immediately, since that would become impractical and costly due to share price volatility and transaction costs. This is also the pattern if companies were to target interest coverage: Share prices are ultimately driven by future operating earnings and cash flows. If share prices rise and remain there, earnings and cash flows eventually will rise, and that is probably when companies start to increase leverage.

Although leverage and coverage ratios both point in the same direction, interest coverage targets are more appropriate for setting long-term capital structure targets. One reason is that coverage measures credit quality more accurately (see the discussion of leverage and coverage in this chapter). A second reason is that leverage would be a moving target as share prices fluctuate. Coverage can be more readily applied when making long-term capital structure analyses, because it does not require any valuation estimate going forward but simply interest and EBITDA. The final reason is that some companies are more conservative whereas others are more aggressive in setting capital structure targets. More conservative companies are more likely to prefer equity-based financing because more conservative firms have less risk tolerance. Also, more conservative firms are more likely to select long-term financing alternatives over short-term financing alternatives.

24

Investor Communications

1. C

2. A

3. D

4. C

5. C

6. A. True
   B. True
   C. False
   D. False
   E. True

7. A. True
   B. True
   C. False
   D. True
   E. False

8. A. A systematic approach helps executives communicate with investors more effectively and efficiently.

B. The objective of investor relations should be the alignment of share price and intrinsic value. It should not focus on trying to maximize the share price. A systematic approach can help align the market price of a company's shares with the company's intrinsic value.

9. A. The communication strategy should be grounded in a thoughtful analysis of market value relative to management's careful estimate of intrinsic value.

   B. The investment story is consistent with the firm's underlying strategy and performance.

   C. It has transparency about performance and the drivers of value (with some exceptions). Transparency includes providing operating measures that the company uses to run its business, as well as financial results.

10. In corporate investor communications, transparency is the free flow of publicly available information. That information should be properly and fully identified, described adequately and accurately, and properly classified. Managers should apply transparency guidelines consistently to parent and subsidiaries, domestic and foreign subsidiaries, affiliates and related entities over which the company has significant influence in order to prevent companies from manipulating financial information.

25

Taxes

1. True

2. False

3. True

4. True

5. True

6. False

7. True

8. False

9.

Account	DTA or DTL?	Operating or nonoperating?
Nondeductible intangibles	DTL	Nonoperating
Tax loss carry-forwards	DTA	Nonoperating
Accelerated depreciation	DTL	Operating
Pension and postretirement benefits	DTA	Nonoperating
Warranty reserves	DTA	Operating

10.

	Domestic subsidiary	Foreign subsidiary	R&D tax credits	One-time credits	Company
EBITA	3,000	800			3,800
Amortization	(1,000)	(200)			(1,200)
EBIT	2,000	600			2,600
Interest expense	(800)	(200)			(1,000)
Gains on asset sales	100	0			100
Earnings before taxes	1,300	400			1,700
Taxes	(390)	(160)	110	88	(352)
Net income	910	240			1,150
Tax rates (percent)					
Statutory rate	30%	40%			
Effective tax rate					20.7%
EBITA	3,000	800			3,800
Operating taxes	(900)	(320)	110		(1,110)
NOPLAT	2,100	480	110		2,690
Tax rates (percent)					
Statutory rate	30%	40%			
Operating tax rate					29.2%

26

Nonoperating Expenses, One-Time Charges, Reserves, and Provisions

1. A. No
   B. Yes
   C. No
   D. No
   E. Yes
   F. Yes
   G. No
   H. No
   I. No

2. **NOPLAT**

Reported EBITA	$4,000
Interest associated with plant decommissioning	500
Increase in income smoothing reserve	600
NOPLAT	$5,100

Invested Capital

Reserve for plant decommissioning	$ 5,000
Reserve for restructuring	1,000
Reserve for income smoothing	2,500
Equity	10,000
Invested capital	$18,500

ROIC = $5,100/$18,500 = 27.57%

3.

Balance sheet	Year 1	Year 2	Year 3
Starting reserve	0	30.80	64.07
Plant-decommissioning expense	30.80	30.80	30.80
Interest cost	0	2.47	5.13
Decommissioning payout	0	0	(100)
Ending reserve	30.80	64.07	0
Income statement			
Reported provision	30.80	33.27	35.93

4. FASB 142 and IFRS 3 require that acquisition premiums be separated into goodwill and intangible assets. In-process R&D is an intangible asset of indefinite life.

5. If a company routinely has to defend itself against litigation, then the charges should be operating charges. An example would likely be in the service industry, most notably a hospital, which may frequently have to defend itself against litigation.

6. It is recommended to treat goodwill impairments as nonoperating and then add back cumulative impairments to goodwill on the balance sheet. Since the purpose of computing ROIC with goodwill is to measure historical performance, including all past acquisition premiums, goodwill should remain at its original level.

7. Whether to make an adjustment to NOPLAT for such an expense depends on whether the charge is large enough to affect perceptions of performance. Making the effort to adjust NOPLAT is recommended only if the adjustment is significant. It is not recommended to make adjustments if they are small, because such adjustments could make the analysis overly complex and time-consuming.

8.

Examples of provisions and reserves	Classification treatment	Treatment in NOPLAT	Treatment in invested capital	Treatment in valuation
Plant decommissioning costs and unfunded retirement plans	D	E	J or K	P
Provisions for the sole purpose of income smoothing	B	G	L	O
Product returns and warranties	C	H	I	M
Restructuring charges (e.g., expected severance payouts from layoffs)	A	F	J or K	N

27

Leases, Pensions, and Other Obligations

1. B, C, A

2. A profitable company has chosen to lease its assets. This move will artificially *lower* operating profits. It will artificially *increase* capital productivity. With respect to return on assets, it is most likely that it will *increase* ROIC.

3. The analyst's adjustments should *increase* assets, *increase* liabilities, and *increase* operating income.

4. The interest rate for operating lease adjustments is usually lower than the firm's cost of debt. This is because that interest expense is secured with the leased assets.

5. An analyst would probably have to get the information on rental expenses from the company's footnotes because it is usually not explicitly shown as a separate line item on the income statement. The analyst would have to estimate the value of the asset because the value is usually not disclosed.

6. Asset value = $4,000/(0.06 + 1/5) = $4,000/0.26 = $15,384.61$.

7. A. The present value of lease payments method estimates the asset's value as the present value of required lease payments, which can be found in the company's footnotes. It usually undervalues the asset because it ignores the residual value returned at the end of the lease contract.

B. The perpetuity method divides rental expense by the cost of debt. This usually overvalues leases because it implicitly assumes the assets have an infinite life. In the formula used in Question 6, this would mean dividing the rental expense by a small number and increasing the estimated asset's value.

C. The analyst can multiply the rental expense by a capitalization rate. Many analysts in the investment banking industry multiply rental expenses by 8 times to approximate asset value. Although based on reasonable assumptions, the method is very simple and can both overvalue and undervalue the leased assets.

8. A. The use of more operating leases led to agencies awarding lower credit ratings, and both combined to increase the required yields on new public bond issuances.

B. Interest rates on unrated, unsecured debt were explained better by credit statistics adjusted for operating leases.

C. All three groups (investors, lenders, and rating agencies) tend to interpret operating leases the same as traditional debt.

9. To determine return on capital, free cash flow, and leverage consistently, make the following adjustments on the balance sheet: *Add back securitized receivables to the balance sheet* and *make a corresponding increase to short-term debt*. The fees paid for securitizing receivables should be *treated as interest*.

10. Excess pension assets should be treated as *nonoperating*, and unfunded pension liabilities should be treated as *a debt equivalent*. With respect to taxes, valuations should be done *on an after-tax basis*.

11. The amortized prior-year service cost and the amortization of loss are zero.

$$\text{Net periodic cost} = \text{pension service cost} + \text{pension interest cost}$$
$$- \text{expected return on plan assets}$$
$$\$350 = \$150 + \$700 - \$500$$

Revenues	$1,000
Operating costs	(600)
Operating profits (unadjusted)	$400
Revenues	$1,000
Operating costs	(600)
Net periodic cost of pension	350
Pension service cost	(150)
Operating profits (adjusted)	$600

12. A.

Operating assets	$3,000
Operating liabilities	(1,000)
Invested capital	$2,000
Book value of debt	$1,500
Book value of equity	500
	$2,000

B. $WACC_{unadjusted} = 8.625\%$

$$= [900/(1{,}500 + 900)] * 13\% + [1{,}500/(1{,}500 + 900)] * 6\%$$

C.

Operating assets	$3,000
Leases	2,000
Adj. operating assets	$5,000
Operating liabilities	(1,000)
Adj. invested capital	$4,000
Book value of debt	$1,500
Leases	2,000
Book value of equity	500
	$4,000

D. $WACC_{adjusted} = 6.977\%$

$$= [900/(1{,}500 + 900 + 2{,}000)] * 13\%$$
$$+ [1{,}500/(1{,}500 + 900 + 2{,}000)] * 6\%$$
$$+ [2{,}000/(1{,}500 + 900 + 2{,}000)] * 5\%$$

28

Capitalized Expenses

1. In both the case of when R&D is expensed and the case of when it is capitalized, the general pattern of ROIC is the same over time. In both cases, in the early years ROIC will rise dramatically. Initially, ROIC with capitalized R&D will be higher than that with expensed R&D. Very soon, however, ROIC with expensed R&D will become higher. Soon after that, both ROICs stabilize, with expensed R&D typically remaining higher. It can be the case, however, that ROIC with capitalized R&D may start to decline while the ROIC with expensed R&D continues to rise.

2. More value is created from additional growth when ROIC is relatively higher, and more value is created from additional ROIC when growth is relatively higher. Therefore, not knowing the true ROIC can lead to an incorrect focus. Managers may pursue growth strategies, when they should be focusing on increasing ROIC. Furthermore, growth can destroy value if ROIC is below the cost of capital. Therefore, not knowing the true ROIC can actually lead to managers engaging in strategies that destroy value.

3. When increasing the length of life from six years to 12 years, the ROIC falls by about one-fifth in both the case of a constant 5 percent and the case of a constant 15 percent R&D expense as a proportion of revenues. Thus, doubling the length of life has a relatively small effect on the ROIC. In fact, increasing the estimated life beyond an estimated two-year life has a rapidly diminishing effect on ROIC.

4. The pattern of decline in ROIC from extending the estimated life is about the same, proportionally, for the assumed 5 percent of revenues expense rate

and the 15 percent of revenues expense rate. In both cases, ROIC declines at a decreasing rate from each two-year increase in the estimated life. The proportional decline when going from two years to four years is 22.7 percent and 36.1 percent for the 5 percent case and the 15 percent case, respectively. The proportional decline when going from 10 years to 12 years is 4.5 percent and 3.4 percent for the 5 percent case and the 15 percent case, respectively.

The implications are that beyond a certain point, increasing the estimated life has a relatively small effect on ROIC. The most important point is that an analyst should capitalize R&D, but details such as the estimated life may have only a marginal effect.

5.

Year	1	2	3	4
Sales	1,000	1,100	1,210	1,331
Production expenses	(500)	(550)	(605)	(665.5)
R&D	(50)	(55)	(60.5)	(66.55)
Depreciation	(200)	(200)	(202)	(206)
Operating income	250	295	342.5	392.95
Initial capital	2,000	2,000	2,020	2,060
Investment	(200)	(220)	(242)	(266.2)
ROIC	12.50%	14.75%	16.96%	19.08%
Adj. initial capital	2,180	2,212	2,265.8	2,341.72
Adj. depreciation	(218)	(221.2)	(226.58)	(234.17)
Adj. operating income	282	328.8	378.42	431.328
Adj. ROIC	12.94%	14.86%	16.70%	18.42%

29

Inflation

---

1. A. Real
   B. Real
   C. Nominal
   D. Real
   E. Nominal
   F. Real
   G. Real

2. A. Assets and liabilities are recorded at historical cost and not revalued to current levels of currency units.
   B. Nominal year-to-year comparisons and ratio analysis (e.g., ROIC and PP&E/revenue) become meaningless.
   C. Continuing-value cash flows require growth and expected returns to reflect highly variable economic conditions.

3. A. Ensure that the WACC estimates in real terms (WACCR) and nominal terms (WACCN) are defined consistently with the inflation assumptions in each year.
   B. The value driver formula as presented in Chapter 10 should be adjusted when estimating continuing value in real terms. The returns on capital in real-terms projections overestimate the economic returns in the case of positive net working capital. The free cash flow in real terms differs from the cash flow implied by the value driver formula by an amount equal to the annual monetary loss on net working capital.

C. When using the continuing-value formulas, make sure the explicit fore-cast period is long enough for the model to reach a steady state with constant growth rates of free cash flow.

4. A. Real forecasts make it impossible to calculate taxes correctly and easily lead to errors in calculating working capital changes; companies grow in real terms when operating efficiencies improve.

   B. The main downside of using nominal cash flows is that future capital expenditures are difficult to project because the typically stable rela-tionship between revenues and fixed assets does not hold under high inflation. As a result, depreciation charges also are difficult to project.

5. A. Forecast operating performance in real terms.

   B. Build financial statements in nominal terms.

   C. Build financial statements in real terms.

   D. Forecast the future free cash flows in real and nominal terms from the projected income statements and balance sheets.

   E. Estimate DCF value in real and nominal terms.

6. $\text{FCF}^R = (1 - 4\%/10\%) * \$2{,}000 - \$1{,}000 * (1 - 200/300) = \$866.67$

7. The first step is to find the real values, $\text{NWC}^R{}_{t-1}$ and the increase in $\text{NWC}^R{}_t$.

   $\text{NWC}^R{}_{t-1} = 100/2 = 50$

   $\text{NWC}^R{}_t = 200/2.5 = 80$

   Increase in $\text{NWC}^R = 80 - 50 = 30$

   Investment in $\text{NWC}^R{}_t = \text{Increase in NWC}^R + \text{NWC}^R{}_{t-1}(1 - \text{IX}_{t-1}/\text{IX}_t)$

   Investment in $\text{NWC}^R{}_t = 30 + 50 * (1 - 2/2.5) = 40$

8. $\text{WACC}^R = (1 + \text{WACC}^N)/(1 + i) - 1$

   $G^R = g^R - i * (\text{NWC}^R/\text{IC}^R)/(1 + i)$

   $\text{CV}^R = (1 - G^R/\text{ROIC}^R) * (\text{NOPLAT}^R)/(\text{WACC}^R - g^R)$

   $\text{WACC}^R = (1 + 0.21)/(1 + 0.1) - 1 = 0.10$

   $G^R = .04 - 0.1 * (1{,}500/10{,}000)/(1.1) = 0.02636 = 2.636\%$

   $\text{CV}^R = (1 - 0.02636/.06) * (3{,}000)/(.10 - .04) = 28{,}033.33$

9.

	Year 1	Year 2
Sales	2,000	2,100
EBITDA	600	640
Depreciation	400	400
EBITA	200	240
Gross property, plant, and equipment	4,000	4,080
Cumulative depreciation	2,500	2,500
Invested capital	1,500	1,580
EBITDA	600	640
Capital expenditures	400	480
Free cash flow (FCF)	200	160
EBITA growth	—	20%
EBITA/sales	10%	11.43%
Return on invested capital	13.33%	15.19%
FCF growth	—	−20%

10. A.

Pro forma financials	Real forecasts				Cont. value
	1	2	3	4	15
Revenues	1,000	1,050	1,103	1,158	1,292
EBITDA	300	315	331	347	387
Depreciation	(70)	(80)	(84)	(88)	(102)
Operating income	230	235	247	259	285
Tax	(115)	(118)	(123)	(130)	(143)
NOPLAT	115	118	123	130	143
Working capital	200	210	221	232	258
Net PPE (beginning of year)	350	400	420	441	511
Less: Depreciation	(70)	(80)	(84)	(88)	(102)
Plus: Capex	120	100	105	110	107
Net PPE (end of year)	400	420	441	463	517
Invested capital	600	630	662	695	775
EBITDA		315	331	347	387
Less: Tax		(118)	(123)	(130)	(143)
Less: Capex		(100)	(105)	(110)	(107)
Less: Working capital increase		(10)	(11)	(11)	(3)
Free cash flow		88	92	96	135

B.

Pro forma financials	Real forecasts				Cont. value
	1	2	3	4	15
Revenues	1,000	1,575	1,985	2,292	4,374
EBITDA	300	473	595	688	1,312
Depreciation	(70)	(80)	(94)	(113)	(277)
Operating income	230	393	501	575	1,035
Tax	(115)	(196)	(251)	(287)	(518)
NOPLAT	115	196	251	287	518
Working capital	200	315	397	458	875
Net PPE (beginning of year)	350	400	470	565	1,385
Less: Depreciation	(70)	(80)	(94)	(113)	(277)
Plus: Capex	120	150	189	218	364
Net PPE (end of year)	400	470	565	670	1,472
Invested capital	600	785	962	1,129	2,347
EBITDA		473	595	688	1,312
Less: Tax		(196)	251	(287)	(518)
Less: Capex		(150)	(189)	(218)	(364)
Less: Working capital increase		(115)	(82)	(62)	(50)
Free cash flow		11	74	121	381

C.

Pro forma financials	Real forecasts				Cont. value
	1	2	3	4	15
Revenues	1,000	1,050	1,103	1,158	1,292
EBITDA	300	315	331	347	387
Depreciation	(70)	(80)	(84)	(88)	(102)
Operating income	230	235	247	259	285
Tax	(115)	(131)	(139)	(145)	(153)
NOPLAT	115	104	107	114	132
Working capital	200	210	221	232	258
Net PPE (beginning of year)	350	400	420	441	511
Less: Depreciation	(70)	(80)	(84)	(88)	(102)
Plus: Capex	120	100	105	110	107
Net PPE (end of year)	400	420	441	463	517
Invested capital	600	630	662	695	775
EBITDA		315	331	347	387
Less: Tax		(131)	(139)	(145)	(153)
Less: Capex		(100)	(105)	(110)	(107)
Less: Working capital increase		(77)	(46)	(31)	(15)
Free cash flow		7	41	61	112

D.

Unadjusted deflated	Real forecasts				Cont. value
	1	2	3	4	15
Real NOPLAT	115	118	123	130	143
Real free cash flow		88	92	96	135
Invested capital/revenue	.60	.60	.60	.60	.60
ROIC pretax	.38%	37%	37%	37%	37%
ROIC posttax	19%	19%	19%	19%	18%
Nominal					
Real NOPLAT*	115	131	139	145	153
Real free cash flow		7	41	61	112
Invested capital/revenue	0.6	0.5	0.48	0.49	0.54
ROIC pretax	38%	50%	52%	51%	44%
ROIC posttax	19%	25%	26%	25%	22%
Real					
Real NOPLAT*	115	104	107	114	132
Real free cash flow		7	41	61	112
Invested capital/revenue	0.6	0.6	0.6	0.6	0.6
ROIC pretax	38%	37%	37%	37%	37%
ROIC posttax	19%	17%	16%	16%	17%

*Deflated NOPLAT and free cash at inflation index.

11. A. Nominal WACC = (1 + Real WACC) × (1 + Inflation rate) − 1 = 1.08 × 1.05 − 1 = 13%

B. Nominal WACC = (1 + Real growth rate) × (1 + Inflation rate) −1 = 1.01 × 1.05 − 1 = 6%

C.

Results	1	2	3	4	5–14	Cont. value 15
Real WACC	8%	8%	8%	8%		8%
Unadjusted deflated free cash flow		88	92	96		135
Continuing value						1,947
Discount factor		0.926	0.857	0.794		0.34
PV of free cash flow		81	79	77	676	709
Unadjusted deflated DCF	1,621					

Note: Free cash flow for years 1 to 15 is to be taken directly from the free cash flow forecast from Question 6. Continuing value is discounted by the real WACC net of the real growth rate in perpetuity.

D.

Results	1	2	3	4	5–14	Cont. value 15
Nominal WACC	30%	62%	30%	19%		13%
Nominal free cash flow		11	74	121		381
Continuing value						5,559
Discount factor		0.617	0.476	0.401		0.101
PV of free cash flow		7	35	48	553	597
Nominal DCF	1,241					

E.

Results	1	2	3	4	5–14	Cont. value 15
Real WACC	8%	8%	8%	8%		8%
Real free cash flow		7	41	61		112
Continuing value						1,641
Discount factor		0.926	0.857	0.794		0.34
PV of free cash flow		7	35	48	553	597
Real DCF	1,241					

30

Foreign Currency

1. A. Temporal method.
   B. Current method.
   C. Current method.
   D. Inflation-adjusted current method.

2. The analyst will convert each of the projected cash flows in the foreign currency into the domestic currency using the forward rate for that horizon. It is more complex because it involves a conversion for each cash flow. In addition to the extra calculations, forward rates may not exist beyond a certain horizon. This means the analyst must estimate synthetic forward exchange rates using interest rate parity theory. According to that theory, changes in foreign exchange rates follow the ratio of expected inflation rates between two currencies.

3. A. Inflation assumptions underlying cash flow projections in a specific currency need to be consistent with inflation assumptions underlying interest rates in that currency.
   B. Forward exchange rates between two currencies need to be consistent with inflation and interest rate differences between those currencies.
   C. Cash flow projections need to be converted from one currency into another at forward exchange rates.

4. The stock market indexes in many countries do not represent large, diversified portfolios. In most European countries, only 25 to 40 companies account for the majority of their stock markets' total capitalization, and

they are often from a limited range of industries. The table in Exhibit 30.4 from the text shows that the industries in the index can explain between 19 and 62 percent, with an average of 49 percent, of the returns of each of the various indexes.

5. **Monetary Data for Computing the Present Value of a Norwegian Subsidiary of an American Corporation**

	2010	2011	2012	2013	2014	2015
Foreign currency (Norwegian kroner—NOK)						
Cash flows						
Nominal cash flow	300	320	340	365	395	440
Real cash flow	297.03	313.73	333.33	354.37	383.50	427.18
Inflation (percent)	1.00	2.00	2.00	3.00	3.00	3.00
Interest rates (percent)						
Real interest rate	2.00	2.00	2.00	2.00	2.00	2.00
Nominal forward interest rate	3.02	4.04	4.04	5.06	5.06	5.06
Nominal interest yield	3.02	3.53	3.70	4.04	4.24	4.38
Spot exchange rate NOK/USD	5					
Forward exchange rate	4.90	4.86	4.76	4.72	4.62	4.54
Domestic currency (U.S. dollars—USD)						
Interest rates						
Nominal interest yield	5.06	5.06	5.40	5.57	5.88	6.09
Nominal forward interest rate	5.06	5.06	6.09	6.09	7.12	7.12
Real interest rate	3.00	3.00	3.00	3.00	3.00	3.00
Inflation (percent)	2.00	2.00	3.00	3.00	4.00	4.00
Cash flows						
Real cash flow	59.99	64.61	69.33	75.15	82.13	93.28
Nominal cash flow	61.19	65.91	71.41	77.41	85.41	97.01

6. Discounted Cash Flows and Present Value of Subsidiary

NOK discount rate		0.970	0.933	0.897	0.854	0.812	0.773
PV of NOK cash flows		291.21	298.56	304.90	311.55	320.92	340.27
Sum of PV of NOK cash flows	1,867.4						
PV of NOK CFs × Spot rate	373.48						
USD discount rate		0.952	0.906	0.854	0.805	0.751	0.702
PV of NOK CFs × Forward rates		58.24	59.71	60.98	62.31	64.18	68.05
Sum of PV of USD cash flows	373.48						

31

Case Study: Heineken

1. A. Customer segmentation analysis: Estimates the potential market share, growth of sales, and ability to maintain and grow markets. The company segments customers and products by various attributes, then associates those attributes with the various core competencies of the firm to provide goods and services.

   B. Business system analysis: Provides the core competencies and abilities of the firm to meet customer expectations. Issues such as time to market, access to sources of material and labor, cycle time, packaging, and distribution channels are combined to highlight the competitive advantages and disadvantages the firm possesses in its industry.

   C. Industry structure analysis: Provides insight into the cycle of feed-forward and feedback networks at work in the industry analysis of buyer, seller, government, technology, new entrants, and substitute product attributes. This component of the analysis provides the dynamic interrelationships among various industry players.

2. A.

Conservative	Historic 2010	2011	2012	Forecast 2013
Working capital	193.000	231.525	277.83	333.396
Net fixed assets	246.000	296.352	355.622	426.747
Invested capital	439.000	527.877	633.452	760.143
Net investment		88.877	105.575	126.690
Debt	314.000	343.12	411.744	494.093
Equity	125.000	184.757	221.708	266.050
Sales growth		20.00%	20.00%	20.00%
Net sales	1,029.00	1,234.80	1,481.76	1,778.11
Operating expense		(926.1)	(1,111.32)	(1,333.58)
SG&A		(229.673)	(275.607)	(330.729)
Depreciation		(31.20)	(37.44)	(44.928)
Operating income		47.828	57.393	68.871
Taxes on EBIT		(19.131)	(22.957)	(27.548)
Change in deferred tax		2.396	2.875	3.450
NOPLAT		31.092	37.310	44.772
ROIC		5.89%	5.89%	5.89%
Debt/invested capital		65.00%	65.00%	65.00%
Equity/invested capital		35.00%	35.00%	35.00%
Tax rate	−21.62%	40.00%	40.00%	40.00%
Interest rate	5.10%	6.00%	7.00%	7.00%
Growth (investment/capital)		20.25%	20.00%	20.00%
Investment rate (growth/ROIC)		343.72%	339.56%	339.56%
EBIT/sales		3.873%	3.873%	3.873%
Sales/invested capital		2.339	2.339	2.339
Working capital/sales	18.756%	18.750%	18.750%	18.750%
NFA/sales	23.907%	24.000%	24.000%	24.000%
Operating expense/sales	74.344%	75.000%	75.000%	75.000%
SG&A/sales	18.562%	18.600%	18.600%	18.600%
Depreciation/sales	2.527%	2.527%	2.527%	2.527%
Change in deferred tax/sales	0.194%	0.194%	0.194%	0.194%
Free cash flow		(57.785)	(68.265)	(81.918)

B.

Aggressive	Historic 2010	Forecast 2011	2012	2013
Working capital	193.000	270.113	378.158	529.421
Net fixed assets	246.000	345.744	484.042	677.658
Invested capital	439.000	615.857	862.199	1,207.079
Net investment		176.857	246.343	344.880
Debt	314.000	400.307	560.429	784.601
Equity	125.000	215.550	301.770	422.478
Sales growth		40.00%	40.00%	40.00%
Net sales	1,029.000	1,440.600	2,016.840	2,823.576
Operating expense		(1,066.04)	(1,472.29)	(2,061.21)
SG&A		(230.496)	(322.694)	(451.772)
Depreciation		(36.015)	(50.421)	(70.589)
Operating income		108.045	171.431	240.004
Taxes on EBIT		(43.218)	(68.573)	(96.002)
Change in deferred tax		2.795	3.913	5.478
NOPLAT		67.622	106.772	149.48
ROIC		10.98%	12.38%	12.38%
Debt/invested capital		65.00%	65.00%	65.00%
Equity/invested capital		35.00%	35.00%	35.00%
Tax rate	−21.62%	40.00%	40.00%	40.00%
Interest rate	5.10%	6.00%	7.00%	7.00%
Growth (investment/capital)		40.29%	40.00%	40.00%
Investment rate (growth/ROIC)		366.90%	323.01%	323.01%
EBIT/sales		7.500%	8.500%	8.500%
Sales/invested capital		2.339	2.339	2.339
Working capital/sales	18.756%	18.750%	18.750%	18.750%
NFA/sales	23.907%	24.000%	24.000%	24.000%
Operating expense/sales	74.344%	74.000%	73.000%	73.000%
SG&A/sales	18.562%	16.000%	16.000%	16.000%
Depreciation/sales	2.527%	2.500%	2.500%	2.500%
Change in deferred tax/sales	0.194%	0.194%	0.194%	0.194%
Free cash flow		(109.235)	(139.571)	(195.4)

3.

Assumptions		Years 1–3 (%)		Years 4+ (%)	
ROIC		18.00		11.00	
NOPLAT growth		20.00		7.00	
WACC		14.00		12.00	

3-Year Horizon	1	2	3	CV Base
NOPLAT	10.00	12.00	14.40	15.41
Depreciation	2.50	3.00	3.60	
Gross cash flow	12.50	15.00	18.00	
Gross investment	(13.61)	(16.33)	(19.60)	
Free cash flow	(1.11)	(1.33)	(1.60)	
Discount factor	0.88	0.77	0.68	
Present value FCF	(0.97)	(1.03)	(1.08)	
PV FCF 1–3	(3.08)			
PV CV	75.64			
Total value	72.56			

5-Year Horizon	1	2	3	4	5	CV Base
NOPLAT	10.00	12.00	14.40	15.41	16.49	17.64
Depreciation	2.50	3.00	3.60	3.85	4.12	
Gross cash flow	12.50	15.00	18.00	19.26	20.61	
Gross investment	(13.61)	(16.33)	(19.60)	(13.66)	(14.61)	
Free cash flow	(1.11)	(1.33)	(1.60)	5.60	6.00	
Discount factor	0.88	0.77	0.68	0.60	0.54	
Present value FCF	(0.97)	(1.03)	(1.08)	3.38	3.23	
PV FCF 1–3	3.53					
PV CV	69.03					
Total value	72.56					

Value is the same for each horizon. This is only because the calculation for free cash flow, and its associated present value, is consistent for the two cases. For the three-year horizon, and the first three years of the five-year horizon, the calculations are identical. The first two years of the three-year horizon CV base and years 4 and 5 of the five-year horizon are also identical. This can be noted by looking at the free cash flows for the explicit forecast period in the five-year horizon. For years 1 to 3, the negative free cash flows fall from a level of gross investment that exceeds gross cash flow. This in turn results from a growth rate that exceeds the ability of those assets to return a profit during those years. Years 4 and 5 yield free cash flows that are positive. In those years of the explicit forecast, growth is less than return on new investment, which returns a surplus cash flow, just as it does, by assumption, for the CV base year and thereon for what is essentially a growing perpetuity. All that has happened in the valuation is a different split on the same value. For the short-term forecast, the explicit forecast period produces –3.08 in present value with the rest of the 75.64 of continuing base value. The longer-run horizon split is a positive 3.53 for the explicit forecast plus a commensurately lower CV base value of 63.03. Both add up to the same amount, 72.56, because both are effectively using the same cash flow streams.

4.

Assumptions	Years 1–3 (%)			Years 4+ (%)
ROIC	18.00			15.75
Growth	20.00			5.00
WACC	14.00			12.00
3-Year Horizon	**1**	**2**	**3**	**CV Base**
NOPLAT	10.00	12.00	14.40	15.12
Net investment	−11.11	−13.33	−16.00	
Free cash flow	−1.11	−1.33	−1.60	
Beginning invested capital	55.56	66.67	80.00	
Net investment	11.11	13.33	16.00	
New invested capital	66.67	80.00	96.00	
NOPLAT	10.00	12.00	14.40	
Capital charge	−7.78	−9.33	−11.20	
Economic profit	2.22	2.67	3.20	
Discount factor	0.8772	0.7695	0.6750	
Present value FCF	−0.97	−1.03	−1.08	
Present value EP	1.95	2.05	2.16	
PV FCF 1–3	−3.08			
PV CV FCF	99.51			
Total value	96.43			
PV FCF 1–3	6.16			
PV CV	34.71			
Invested capital	55.56			
Total value	96.43			

32

Valuing Flexibility

1. A

2. D

3. B. Since there are no losses to avoid by stopping the project, the NPV is the same with and without flexibility: NPV = $0 = -$10 + 0.5 * $1/0.05 + 0.05 * $0/0.05.

4. C

5. Flexibility reduces the investment risk for this project, but the flexibility is essentially a call option on the project itself. By definition, call options are more risky per dollar invested than the underlying asset; therefore, the valuing of the flexibility requires discounting their future cash flows at higher cost of capital. The total investment risk for the project with flexibility is lower because there is a much lower value exposed if the investment can be deferred.

6. A. Increase in value because: The higher interest rate increases the value of the call option.

   B. Decrease in value because: The higher interest rate decreases the present value of the cash flows.

7. A. What events are the key sources of uncertainty?

   B. What decision can management make in response to events?

   C. What payoffs are linked to these decisions?

8. To value flexibility:

    A. Estimate the standard NPV of the investment project without flexibility, using a traditional discounted cash flow model.

    B. Expand the DCF model into an event tree, mapping how the value of the project evolves over time, using unadjusted probabilities and the weighted average cost of capital.

    C. Turn the event tree into a decision tree by identifying the types of managerial flexibility that are available.

    D. Estimate the contingent NPV using a DTA or ROV approach.

9. Without the option to expand, the expected NPV is:

$$NPV = -\$500 + 0.1 * \$400/0.25 + 0.9 * \$50/0.25$$
$$NPV = -\$160$$

With the option to expand, the expected NPV is:

$$NPV = -\$500 + 0.1 * [\$400/0.25 + 8 * (-\$500 + \$400/0.25)/1.25]$$
$$+ 0.9 * \$50/0.25$$
$$NPV = \$544$$

10. Standard $NPV = -\$243.29 = (0.2 * 0.5) * \$4{,}000/(1.2^2) - \$240 - \$100/1.04$
$$- \$200/(1.04^2)$$

With flexibility, the option to proceed at the end of the research phase is:

$$PV(Option) = Max[PV(Testing) - Inv(Testing), 0]$$
$$PV(Testing) = \$1{,}296.43 = 0.5 * [\$4{,}000/(1.2^2) - \$200/(1.04^2)] + 0.50 * 0$$

The present value of the development project prior to the testing phase is:

$$PV(Option) = \$1{,}200.28 = Max[(\$1{,}296.43 - \$100/1.04), 0]$$

The contingent NPV for the entire project prior to the research phase is:

$$\$0.06 = Max[0.20 * (\$1{,}200.28) + 0.8 * (0) - \$240, 0]$$

33

Valuation in Emerging Markets

1. F, A, E, C, D

2. Although the analyst would use some judgment in estimating the probabilities, there is evidence for determining a range of reasonable values, which is likely to be between 20 and 30 percent.

   The 20 percent number comes from the analysis of changes in GDP of 20 emerging economies over the past 20 years in which it was found they had experienced economic distress about once every five years (a real-terms GDP decline of more than 5 percent).

   The 30 percent number is from a study that found that government default probabilities five years into the future in emerging markets such as Argentina were around 30 percent in nondistress years.

3. A. Use the capital asset pricing model (CAPM) to estimate the cost of equity in emerging markets.

   B. Be flexible in assembling the available information piece by piece to build the cost of capital, and triangulate the results with country risk premium approaches and multiples. In general, be pragmatic because in emerging markets there are often significant information and data gaps.

   C. Be sure monetary assumptions are consistent. Ground your model in a common set of monetary assumptions to ensure that the cash flow forecasts and discount rate are consistent.

D. Allow for changes in the cost of capital. The cost of capital in an emerging-market valuation may change based on evolving inflation expectations, changes in a company's capital structure and cost of debt, or foreseeable reforms in the tax system.

E. Don't mix approaches. Use the cost of capital to discount the cash flows in a probability-weighted scenario approach. Do not add any risk premium, because you would then be double-counting risk. If you are discounting only future cash flows in a business-as-usual scenario, add a risk premium to the discount rate.

4. A. Real GDP growth, price inflation (including consumer prices), wages, interest rates, exchange rates, and whatever other parameters are deemed relevant (e.g., oil prices).

B. The purpose is not so much to create the right economic forecasts, which may not even be possible because of the uncertainty. The goal should be to create one or more sets of consistent assumptions to apply to the valuation.

C. Research has shown that purchasing power parity (PPP) does hold over the long run, even between emerging and developed economies. Thus the analysts should include in the forecasts the assumption that exchange rates ultimately do adjust for differences in inflation between the relevant countries.

5. The expected cash flow for the first year is:

$$\text{Expected first-year cash flow} = 440 = 0.8 * 500 + 0.2 * 200$$

Since the growth rate in both scenarios is 4 percent, the value of the firm is:

$$\text{Value} = 8{,}800 = 440/(0.09 - 0.04)$$

6. The risk premium that is consistent with the answer in Question 5 is the one that will give the same value of the scenario DCF using only the business-as-usual scenario. In other words, it solves the following equation:

$$8{,}800 = 500/(.09 + p - 0.04)$$

Manipulating this algebraically gives:

$$p = 0.00682 = 500/8{,}800 - 0.09 + 0.04$$

or 0.682%.

34

Valuing High-Growth Companies

1. A. Penetration rates.

   B. Average revenue per customer.

   C. Sustainable gross margins.

2. A. Monte Carlo simulation.

   B. Real options.

   C. Probability-weighted scenarios. This is the recommended method because it makes the critical assumptions and interactions more transparent.

3. The scenario weights should be based on a fundamental economic analysis for determining value (e.g., market size, market share, and competitor margins). Those estimates should be calibrated against the historical performance of other high-growth companies.

4. A probability-weighted scenario can highlight the economic issues driving a company's value. Using just a few scenarios makes critical assumptions and interactions more transparent than other modeling approaches. One can use scenario analysis to determine the value impact of changes in individual drivers.

5. The analyst should focus on sizing the future market of the start-up company, predicting the level of profitability, and estimating the investments

necessary to achieve success. To do this, the analyst would choose a point well into the future at a time when financial performance is likely to stabilize, begin forecasting, and then work backward to link the forecast to current performance. Measures of current performance are likely to commingle investments and expenses, so when possible the analyst should capitalize hidden investments (even those expensed under traditional accounting rules). It is not advised to rely on a single long-term forecast. The analyst should describe the market's development in terms of multiple scenarios, including total size, ease of competitive entry, and so on. When building a comprehensive scenario, the analyst should be sure all forecasts, including revenue growth, profitability margins, and required investment, are consistent with the underlying assumptions of the particular scenario. Finally, probabilistic weights should be applied to each scenario. The weights must be consistent with long-term historical evidence on corporate growth.

6.

Scenario	Intrinsic value ($ million)	Probability	Intrinsic value x probability
Success in both domestic and international markets	2,500	0.3	750
Success in domestic market	1,500	0.5	750
Failure in domestic market	700	0.2	140
Expected intrinsic value			1,640
Shares outstanding: 200 million		Expected share price	82

7.

Scenario	Intrinsic value ($ million)	Probability	Intrinsic value x Probability
Success in both domestic and international markets	2,500	0.2	500
Success in domestic market	1,500	0.5	750
Failure in domestic market	700	0.3	210
Expected intrinsic value			1,460
Shares outstanding: 200 million		Expected share price	73

The price changes by over 10 percent with different probabilities. Using the initial forecast as a base:

$$\text{Percent change} = (82 - 73)/82 = 10.98\%$$

Computing the percent change by weighting each set of scenarios equally, using the log/ratio method, gives:

$$\text{Percent change} = \ln(82/73) = 11.63\%$$

Thus, changing only two of the smaller percentages can have a sizable impact on the estimated share price.

35

Valuing Cyclical Companies

1. $PV_0(FCF) = 10 + NPV(10\%, 20, 40, 30, 10) + NPV(10\%, 20, 40, 30, 10)/(1.1^4 - 1) = 264.30$

   $PV_1(FCF) = 10 + NPV(10\%, 20, 40, 30, 10) + NPV(10\%, 20, 40, 30, 10)/(1.1^4 - 1) = 279.73$

   $PV_2(FCF) = 10 + NPV(10\%, 20, 40, 30, 10) + NPV(10\%, 20, 40, 30, 10)/(1.1^4 - 1) = 285.70$

   $PV_3(FCF) = 10 + NPV(10\%, 20, 40, 30, 10) + NPV(10\%, 20, 40, 30, 10)/(1.1^4 - 1) = 270.27$

   Since four numbers in each case exhaust all possible outcomes, the population standard deviation method should be used.

   The standard deviation of the FCFs is 11.18.
   The standard deviation of the PV of the FCFs is 8.27.

2. A. 3
   B. 1
   C. 2
   D. 4

3. C

4. D

5. A.

	2006	2007	2008	2009	2010
Invested capital statement					
Working capital	831	125	(104)	(3)	368
Long-term assets	9,740	10,203	10,034	10,055	12,338
Operating invested capital	10,571	10,328	9,930	10,052	12,706
Net investment		(243)	(398)	122	2,654
Debt	7,052	6,817	6,460	6,928	8,831
Equity	3,519	3,511	3,470	3,124	3,875
NOPLAT statement					
Sales	14,313	13,024	13,094	13,342	17,977
Operating expense	(9,794)	(9,798)	(10,209)	(10,231)	(13,333)
General expense	(1,406)	(1,475)	(1,296)	(1,204)	(1,670)
Depreciation	(984)	(996)	(1,017)	(997)	(1,013)
EBIT	2,129	755	572	910	1,961
Taxes on EBIT	(852)	(350)	(346)	(386)	(759)
Change in deferred taxes	10	14	100	38	73
NOPLAT	1,287	419	326	562	1,275
Provision for income taxes	679	135	106	202	705
Tax shield on interest expense	173	213	282	188	192
Tax on investment income	–	–	(78)	(10)	(137)
Tax on nonoperating income	–	2	36	6	–
Taxes on EBIT	852	350	346	386	759
Net income statement					
Sales	14,313	13,024	13,094	13,342	17,977
Operating expense	(9,794)	(9,798)	(10,209)	(10,231)	(13,333)
General expense	(1,406)	(1,475)	(1,296)	(1,204)	(1,670)
Depreciation	(984)	(996)	(1,017)	(997)	(1,013)
EBIT	2,129	755	572	910	1,961
Investment income	–	–	128	24	355
Investment expense	(432)	(459)	(465)	(443)	(495)
Miscellaneous, net	–	(5)	(60)	(15)	–
Earnings before taxes	1,697	291	175	476	1,821
Income taxes	(679)	(135)	(106)	(202)	(705)
Net income (before extra items)	1,018	156	69	274	1,116
Tax rate	40%	46%	61%	42%	39%
Reconciliation to net income statement					
Net income	1,018	156	69	274	1,116
Add: Increase in deferred taxes	10	14	100	38	73
Adjusted net income	1,028	170	169	312	1,189
Add: Interest expense after tax	259	246	183	255	303
Income available to investors	1,287	416	352	567	1,492
Less: Interest income after tax	–	–	(50)	(14)	(218)

	2006	2007	2008	2009	2010
Less: Nonop. income after tax	–	3	24	9	–
NOPLAT	1,287	419	326	562	1,275
ROIC tree					
ROIC		4.0%	3.2%	5.7%	12.7%
= (1 – EBIT cash tax rate)		55.5%	56.9%	61.7%	65.0%
× Pretax ROIC		7.1%	5.5%	9.2%	19.5%
= EBIT/sales		5.8%	4.4%	6.8%	10.9%
× Sales/invested capital		1.23	1.27	1.34	1.79
EBIT/sales = 1 – (Operating expense/sales		75.2%	78.0%	76.7%	74.2%
+ General expense/sales		11.3%	9.9%	9.0%	9.3%
+ Depreciation/sales)		7.6%	7.8%	7.5%	5.6%
Sales/invested capital					
= 1/(Op. working capital/sales		6.4%	1.0%	(0.8%)	0.0%
+ Long-term op. assets/sales)		74.8%	77.9%	75.2%	55.9%
Change in deferred tax/sales		0.107%	0.764%	0.285%	0.406%
Free cash flow statement					
NOPLAT		419	326	562	1,275
Depreciation		996	1,017	997	1,013
Gross cash flow		1,415	1,343	1,559	2,288
Increase in op. working capital		(706)	(229)	101	371
Capital expenditures		1,459	848	1,018	3,296
Gross investment		753	619	1,119	3,667
Free cash flow		662	724	440	(1,379)
Nonoperating cash flow		(5)	68	9	355
Cash flow available to investors		657	792	449	(1,024)
Cost of capital					
Beta		1.33	1.33	1.33	1.33
Debt/invested capital		66.7%	66.0%	65.1%	68.9%
Equity/invested capital		33.3%	34.0%	34.9%	31.1%
Cost of debt		6.5%	6.8%	6.9%	7.1%
Cost of equity		15.0%	15.0%	15.0%	15.0%
Weighted average cost of capital		7.3%	6.9%	7.8%	7.7%
Economic profit					
NOPLAT		418.7	325.5	561.8	1,274.80
Capital charge		(772.8)	(708.9)	(774.4)	(771.0)
Economic profit		(354)	(383.3)	(212.6)	503.8

	Average 2006–2010	FY 2011	FY 2012	FY 2013	CV 2014
Working capital	243,400	254,752	266,634	279,070	—
Net fixed assets	10,474,000	10,962,507	11,473,798	12,008,935	—
Invested capital	10,717,400	11,217,259	11,740,431	12,288,005	12,861,117
Net investment		499,859	523,172	547,573	573,112
Debt	7,217,600	7,554,229	7,906,557	8,275,319	8,661,279
Equity	3,499,800	3,663,031	3,833,874	4,012,686	4,199,837
Sales growth		4.66%	4.66%	4.66%	
Net sales	14,350,000	15,019,283	15,719,782	16,452,952	
Operating expense		(11,170,788)	(11,691,793)	(12,237,098)	
General expense		(1,475,972)	(1,544,811)	(1,616,861)	
Depreciation		(1,048,105)	(1,096,989)	(1,148,152)	
EBIT		1,324,418	1,386,189	1,450,841	
Taxes on EBIT		(512,748)	(536,663)	(561,693)	
Change in deferred tax		58,654	61,389	64,253	
Net op. profit less adjusted tax		870,324	910,915	953,400	997,867
Net investment		(499,859)	(523,172)	(547,573)	(573,112)
Free cash flow		370,465	387,743	405,827	424,755
Cost of capital		7.46%	7.46%	7.46%	7.46%
Economic profit		70,822	74,125	77,582	81,201
Beta	1.37	1.368	1.368	1.368	1.368
Unlevered beta	0.6043	0.5827	0.5827	0.5827	0.5827
PV factors	1	0.93058	0.86598	0.80586	
	PV sums				
PV short-term forecast	1,007,566	344,747	335,777	327,041	
Continuing value				15,192,342	
PV continuing value	12,242,951				
Market value of assets	13,250,516				
Debt	(7,217,600)				
Market value of equity	6,032,916				
Number of shares	172.3				
Stock price	35.01				
	Sum				
PV economic profit 1–3	192,617	65,906	64,191	62,521	
Continuing value				2,904,337	
PV continuing value	2,340,499				
Invested capital	10,717,400				

	Average 2006–2010	FY 2011	FY 2012	FY 2013	CV 2014
Market value of assets	13,250,516				
ROIC	6.36%	8.12%	8.12%	8.12%	8.12%
Debt/invested capital	**67.34%**	**67.34%**	**67.34%**	**67.34%**	**67.34%**
Equity/invested capital	32.66%	32.66%	32.66%	32.66%	32.66%
Tax rate	**38.71%**	**38.71%**	**38.71%**	**38.71%**	**38.71%**
Interest rate	**6.83%**	**6.83%**	**6.83%**	**6.83%**	**6.83%**
Growth (investment/capital)		**4.66%**	**4.66%**	**4.66%**	**4.66%**
Investment rate (growth/ROIC)		57.43%	57.43%	57.43%	57.43%
EBIT/sales		8.82%	8.82%	8.82%	
Sales/invested capital		1.4014	1.4014	1.4014	
Working capital/sales	1.6962%	1.6962%	1.6962%	1.6962%	
NFAOA/sales	72.9895%	72.9895%	72.9895%	72.9895%	
Operating expense/ sales	74.3763%	74.3763%	74.3763%	74.3763%	74.3763%
SG&A/sales	9.8272%	9.8272%	9.8272%	9.8272%	9.8272%
Depreciation/sales	6.9784%	6.9784%	6.9784%	6.9784%	6.9784%
Change in deferred tax/sales	0.3910%	0.3910%	0.3910%	0.3910%	0.3910%

B.

	Average 2006–2010	FY 2011	FY 2012	FY 2013	CV 2014
Working capital	243,400	258,004	273,484	289,893	–
Net fixed assets	10,474,000	11,102,440	11,768,586	12,474,702	–
Invested capital	10,717,400	11,360,444	12,042,071	12,764,595	13,359,935
Net investment		643,044	681,627	722,524	595,340
Debt	7,217,600	7,650,656	8,109,695	8,596,277	8,997,207
Equity	3,499,800	3,709,788	3,932,375	4,168,318	4,362,728
Sales growth		6.00%	6.00%	6.00%	
Net sales	14,350,000	15,211,000	16,123,660	17,091,080	
Operating expense		(11,104,030)	(11,770,272)	(12,476,488)	
General expense		(1,494,812)	(1,584,501)	(1,679,571)	
Depreciation		(1,061,484)	(1,125,173)	(1,192,683)	
EBIT		1,550,674	1,643,714	1,742,337	
Taxes on EBIT		(600,343)	(636,364)	(674,546)	
Change in deferred tax		59,402	62,967	66,745	
Net op. profit less adj. tax		1,009,733	1,070,317	1,134,536	1,187,451
Net investment		(643,044)	(681,627)	(722,524)	(595,340)
Free cash flow		366,689	388,690	412,012	592,111
Cost of capital		7.46%	7.46%	7.46%	7.46%
Economic profit		210,232	222,846	236,216	235,232
Beta	1.37	1.368	1.368	1.368	1.368
Unlevered beta	0.6043	0.5827	0.5827	0.5827	0.5827
PV factors	1	0.93058	0.86598	0.80586	
	PV sums				
PV short-term forecast	1,009,857	341,234	336,598	332,025	
Continuing value				21,178,205	
PV continuing value	17,066,738				
Market value of assets	18,076,594				
Debt	(7,217,600)				
Market value of equity	10,858,994				
Number of shares	172.3				
Stock price	63.02				

	Average 2006–2010	FY 2011	FY 2012	FY 2013	CV 2014
	Sum				
PV economic profit 1–3	**578,975**	195,637	192,980	190,358	
Continuing value				8,413,610	
PV continuing value	**6,780,219**				
Invested capital	**10,717,400**				
Market value of assets	18,076,594				
ROIC	6.36%	9.42%	9.42%	9.42%	9.30%
Debt/invested capital	**67.34%**	**67.34%**	**67.34%**	**67.34%**	**67.34%**
Equity/invested capital	32.66%	32.66%	32.66%	32.66%	32.66%
Tax rate	**38.71%**	**38.71%**	**38.71%**	**38.71%**	**38.71%**
Interest rate	**6.83%**	**6.83%**	**6.83%**	**6.83%**	**6.83%**
Growth (investment/capital)		**6.00%**	**6.00%**	**6.00%**	**4.66%**
Investment rate (growth/ROIC)		63.68%	63.68%	63.68%	50.14%
EBIT/sales		10.19%	10.19%	10.19%	
Sales/invested capital		1.4193	1.4193	1.4193	
Working capital/ sales	1.70%	1.70%	1.70%	1.70%	
NFAOA/sales	72.99%	72.99%	72.99%	72.99%	
Operating expense/sales	74.38%	73.00%	73.00%	73.00%	73.00%
SG&A/sales	9.83%	9.83%	9.83%	9.83%	9.83%
Depreciation/sales	6.98%	6.98%	6.98%	6.98%	6.98%
Change in deferred tax/sales	0.39%	0.39%	0.39%	0.39%	0.39%

36

Valuing Banks

1. B

2. D

3. C

4. C

5. A. Other
   B. Trading
   C. Other
   D. Other
   E. Trading
   F. Trading
   G. Trading

6.

	1988	2007
Commission income	2	2
Interest income	1	1
Trading income	3	3
Other	4	4

Although the rankings have not changed, the relative importance of these four income sources has changed radically over the past two decades. Most notably, European banks have steadily shifted away from interest income toward commission and trading income.

7. A.

Interest income	$67.00
Interest expense	(15.20)
Other expenses	(30.00)
Net profit before taxes	$21.80
Taxes	(8.72)
Net income	$13.08

B.

Loan spread	$40.20
Deposit spread	15.20
Equity spread	1.6
Reserve debt	(5.20)
Expenses	(30.0)
Net profit before taxes	$21.8
Taxes	(8.72)
Net income	$13.08

C. The two approaches are equivalent. The following is a proof of this equivalence. It starts with the regular income statement equation for net income:

$$\text{NI} = (r_L \times L - r_D \times D - E) \times (1 - T)$$

where r_L and r_D are the loan and deposit rates, E is the noninterest expense, and T is the marginal tax rate.

For the spread model:

$$NI = [(r_L - r_M) \times L + (r_M - r_D) \times D + r_M \times S - r_M \times R - E] \times (1 - T)$$

where r_M = the money rate of return.

The next step is to recall the balance sheet relationship:

$$R + L = D + S$$

or

$$D + S - R - L = 0$$

where R = Cash reserve
L = Loans
D = Deposits
S = Equity

Gathering the terms in r_M in the spread model gives:

$$NI = [r_L \times L - r_D \times D + r_M \times (D + S - R - L) - E)] \times (1 - T)$$
$$NI = [r_L \times L - r_D \times D - E] \times (1 - T)$$

The result is the same as the income model from the financial statements. In constructing the spread model, banks use an assumed yield, the money rate, to benchmark the profitability of loans and deposits and debit the lack of earning ability of cash reserves at the Federal Reserve. The equality of the two methods depends on the same rate being used as a proxy for the cost of equity capital. There can be a problem when using this rate to benchmark loans and deposits and the cost of equity. Each of these items has a different risk-adjusted cost of capital, and thus a different benchmark. The money rate is not necessarily related to the equity cost of capital and can be reliably assigned only to the cash reserve account. Allocations based on the spread model must be viewed with caution since they do not represent comparisons of investments (short and long) with their risk-adjusted opportunity costs of capital.

8.

Cash flow statement forecasts	2011	2012	2013	2014	2015
Net income	73	77	81	85	88
(Increase) decrease in equity	−90	−90	−10	−11	−11
Other comprehensive income (loss)	−1	0	1	2	2
Cash flow to equity	−18	−13	72	76	79
				$CV_{2015} =$	1,087.5
Cash flow value	−18	−13	72	76	1,166.5
PV(CFE) = 879.11					

$$CV = \frac{90\left(1 - \dfrac{0.02}{0.10}\right)}{0.08 - 0.02} + \frac{2 - 11}{0.08} = 1087.5$$

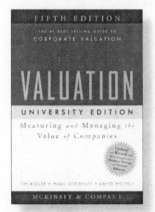
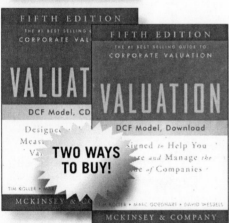
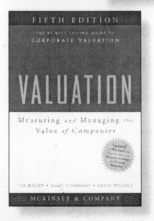